Desert in a Reparative Frame

Desert in a Reparative Frame

Re-Defining Contemporary Criminal Justice

David J. Cornwell

eleven
international publishing

Published, sold and distributed by Eleven International Publishing
P.O. Box 85576
2508 CG The Hague
The Netherlands
Tel.: +31 70 33 070 33
Fax: +31 70 33 070 30
e-mail: sales@elevenpub.nl
www.elevenpub.com

Sold and distributed in USA and Canada
International Specialized Book Services
920 NE 58th Avenue, Suite 300
Portland, OR 97213-3786, USA
Tel.: 1-800-944-6190 (toll-free)
Fax: +1 503 280-8832
orders@isbs.com
www.isbs.com

Eleven International Publishing is an imprint of Boom uitgevers Den Haag.

ISBN 978-94-6236-644-2
ISBN 978-94-6274-464-6 (E-book)

Printed in The Netherlands

For Jeanie

'Agnosco veteris vestigia flammae.'
Virgil, *Aeneid*, IV, 23

Table of Contents

Acknowledgements

There are a number of people whom I would like to thank for making completion and publication of this book possible. Professors John Blad of Erasmus University, in Rotterdam, the Netherlands, and Anni Hesselink of the University of South Africa, Pretoria, have both encouraged this work from its tentative beginnings, and maintained valued friendships over the past decade for which I am deeply grateful.

Emeritus Professor Lode Walgrave of the KU Leuven University in Belgium has, over many years past, striven to promote restorative justice to its rightful place in the mainstream of criminological discourse. His scholarship has justly attracted a worldwide reputation for its penetrating visions of better justice and social cohesiveness. I am greatly indebted to him for making the time in a still hectic work schedule to write the foreword for this book.

To Selma Hoedt, Sandra van der Molen, Joris Bekkers, Barbara Reed and their colleagues at Eleven International Publishing in The Hague, the Netherlands, I express particular thanks for the efficient and friendly way in which publication of this book has been handled and achieved, and also for the suggestions and advice they have provided in relation to its final structure, copy-editing and presentation. Their assistance has been very much appreciated.

Finally, it would be remiss not to mention the many other friends and colleagues, both academics and practitioners, with whom contacts have been made and ideas exchanged within and across the criminal justice world over recent years. Though too numerous to mention individually, they have all contributed to this and my previous works through their insights and conversations. Their generosity in sharing their knowledge and wisdom has been a sustaining influence for which I am humbly grateful.

About the Author

Dr David J. Cornwell is a consultant criminologist, a former prison governor and tutor at HM Prison Service College Wakefield, United Kingdom. He has wide experience as a practitioner of custodial corrections in both the public and private sectors in the UK and at Bloemfontein in the Republic of South Africa. He is the author of four books on restorative justice: *Criminal punishment and Restorative Justice* (2006), *Doing Justice Better* (2007), *The Penal Crisis and the Clapham Omnibus* (2009), and *Mercy: A Restorative Philosophy* (2014), and of numerous journal articles and conference papers. With John Blad and Martin Wright he was also the co-editor of *Civilising Criminal Justice* (2014).

David Cornwell has undertaken consultancy assignments under the auspices of the Council of Europe in Poland (Themis Plan), and visited prisons in a number of European and other countries worldwide. His final appointment prior to leaving HM Prison Service was as Head of Security Audit in the Standards Audit Unit, in which capacity he visited and assessed the security arrangements of more than 80 prisons within England and Wales between 1995 and 1997. He subsequently worked for Group 4 in the private sector until 2004 when he retired to focus on writing about criminology.

The Author of the Foreword

Professor Dr Lode Walgrave is Emeritus Professor in Criminology at the KU Leuven in Belgium. He is a founding member and was chair of the International Network for Research on Restorative Justice and of the International Association for Criminology of Youth. He has researched and written in the field of restorative justice extensively, and it was through his initiative that the Belgian government introduced restorative justice in the reformed Belgian Youth Justice Act from 2006 after a trial period by means of an action research project.

He has contributed chapters to many of the most recent international readers on restorative justice, and among his many publications his book *Restorative Justice, Self-Interest and Responsible Citizenship* (2008) stands out as a landmark work attracting wide international acclaim. In 2008, Lode Walgrave received the European Criminology Award.

Author's Preface

Writing this book has proved to be a challenging experience. Some thirty-five years spent in initial study of, subsequent working within, and eventually observing the penal processes of England and Wales and of a number of other countries has changed many perspectives of how these processes actually administer and deliver justice.

Latterly, I have concluded that the Anglo-Saxon tradition of justice administration upon which many Western-style countries have founded their own penal systems resembles a jigsaw in which the individual pieces fail to fit together precisely. The result is evident in a blurred and sometimes confusing image that is widely imagined to have a clear definition and purpose. Many conversations with academic and practitioner colleagues have confirmed this impression to a disturbing extent.

My search to discover why this situation should exist has led to the conclusion that the jigsaw has at least one misshapen piece that has distorted its image, and that this piece represents the concept of desert. Yet desert has long been perceived as having an unequivocal and taken-for-granted status of an almost unquestionable nature within the philosophy of criminal punishment. Offences transgress the law and cause harm: both the transgression and the harm deserve punishment; and the punishment requites both. The proposition, it is claimed, is thus simple, logical and beyond reasonable dispute.

This book challenges such a proposition, its apparent simplicity, its logic and its conclusion to a profound extent, if only because other explanations of desert are not merely possible, but may even be preferable if true justice is to be delivered. It is a work argued from first principles, but with a utilitarian rather than a solely retributive perspective. Its explanations are offered in an attempt to pave the way towards a more humane, constructive and inclusive process of justice within contemporary democracies. In so doing, it identifies all the legitimate stakeholders in criminal justice: the state, offenders, victims of crime and communities, some of whose claims and interests have, for too long, been overlooked and neglected.

The work is based upon the prevailing situation within the criminal justice process of England and Wales, one which has evident shortcomings. The same defects are, however, present to a greater or lesser extent within many Western-style democracies across the contemporary world: some of historical origin, but others the direct result of deliberate government policy selection. Its discussions form a journey on which I hope the reader may wish to embark, and follow a path that has hitherto been largely uncharted. Its destination is, quite simply, better justice for all.

David J. Cornwell

Conderton, Tewkesbury, UK
October 2015

Foreword

Lode Walgrave

David Cornwell is one of those scholars who understand that restorative justice is about far more than a series of techniques, a model of responding to offending. He is fully aware that thinking differently about doing justice is based on another view of social relations and even on a particular social ethical approach. Indeed, giving priority to restoring the suffering caused by crime and harm instead of keeping the punitive premise; promoting respectful dialogue among the stakeholders in the aftermath of an offence instead of relying on the authoritative sentencing machine: both witness another fundamental belief. It questions the traditional basic concepts and leads to other attitudes in place of conflict, injustice and crime. In that sense, David Cornwell has in recent years enriched the reflection on restorative justice with original and thought-provoking views.

The author is a diver to sound and to explore the depth under the idea of restorative justice. One of the recent results of his exploration was presented in a book edited together with his companions John Blad and Martin Wright on *Civilizing Criminal Justice* (2013). A year later he published a short book on the concept of mercy. The position is that 'within the context of criminal justice mercy has to be redefined beyond the status of a "virtue" to that of a philosophical and operational component of true justice' (Cornwell, 2014a: 113). And, '... this could only be achieved within a restorative philosophy of justice...' (2014: 47). Cornwell's position reminds one of the distinction made by Nussbaum between the vision of Plato on justice and that of Aristotle (1993). Plato advanced '*dikè*', the strict retributive approach, which 'knows neither equity nor grace, but only cares for strict and simple justice' (Nussbaum, 1993: 219). Aristotle based his vision of justice on '*epieikeia*', which recognises 'imperfect human efforts and complex obstacles to doing well' (Id.), and leads to 'equity, mercy and more constructive ways of responding to crime' (1993: 248). Clearly, Cornwell is an Aristotelian.

Mercy is more flexible and person oriented. This seems however to infect the concept of just desert. Just desert is balanced, proportioned to the wrong committed, and it assures equal treatment of all those who have committed the same offence in the same circumstances. That is only just. Cornwell had to deal with the challenge issued by the just desert concept to the need for mercy. The book in hand is the result. The aim is to uncouple desert from its retributive context and to include it into a reparative frame. He does this by extending the focus of just desert from the offender towards including also the victim and the community as deserving a just response to the act. This book again presents stimulating and challenging ideas and visions. They are argued and documented with rich data, broad erudition, deep experience and great wisdom. They provoke reflection. This is what came first to my mind.

Just desert is embedded in an intuition of reciprocity. If one unjustly inflicts damage or suffering on another and/or community life, he deserves to undergo a pain which is proportionate to the losses he has caused himself. It is supposed that things are evened out then. The problem with this approach to retribution is that reciprocity is expressed in negative terms. Harms are balanced by counter harms. The consequence is that, as Martin Wright once observed, it 'only adds to the total amount of harm in the world' (Wright, 1992: 525). Suffering may be equally (justly) spread, but doubled.

We can, on the contrary, consider retribution in a more constructive sense. 'Because crime hurts, justice should heal' (Braithwaite 2005: 296). In 2006 the grandmother of a three-year-old child killed in a racist shoot out in Antwerp said: 'Confronted with so much hate, we need a huge amount of love'. When harm has been caused, the priority is not to inflict more harm, but to try to take harm away. That is what restorative justice tries to do. I have called this 'inverted constructive retributivism' (Walgrave 2008: 60). Howard Zehr also sees much commonality in restorative justice and retribution. Common to both are: '... a basic moral intuition that a balance has been thrown off by a wrongdoing. Consequently, the victim deserves something and the offender owes something... . There must be a proportional relationship between the act and the response' (Zehr, 2002: 59). Causing harm leads to the obligation to repair. Committing a wrong must be followed by doing good. Maybe it is not so much a 'just desert' that the offender has brought down on himself by his act, but rather a 'just obligation' (or 'just owing') that he has loaded upon himself.

Currently, a trend called 'positive criminology' is emerging (Schuilenberg, Van Staden & Oude Breuil, 2014; Ronel & Segev, 2015). It is a criminology that believes in the positive strengths of humans and aims at a kind of prevention and a type of response that emphasises more what unites than what separates or threatens. It is meant as a response to the predominant approaches in criminal policy and in criminology of the recent decennia, which mainly play 'at the defence', based on mutual mistrust, increasing control and exclusion. These approaches are detrimental to the quality of democracy, to social life and to solidarity.

Restorative justice certainly is part of this 'positive criminology'. It is based on trust. It believes that, if the adequate conditions are provided for, many victims and offenders are prepared and able to meet, and find solutions to the problem caused by crime which are also constructive for social life in general. Practice and research show that this belief is not naïve. Trust is the central component in social capital, which is crucial to making democracy work (Putnam 1993). Without trust, we risk hiding in fortresses of mutual distrust, leading to a halt in the democratic game. Trust is not naïve. Restorative justice gives priority, gives the full chance of inclusive deliberation, but it does not exclude the use of coercion and concern for public safety. But not as starting point: only as a last resort.

David Cornwell's work also witnesses trust in fellow humans without being naïve, giving priority to mercy without denying the need for coercion, reconsidering just Desert in a Reparative Frame, relying on good legal arrangements without being rigid. Calling him a truly 'positive criminologist' is his just desert.

References

Braithwaite, J., 'Between Proportionality and Impunity: Confrontation – Truth – Prevention', *Criminology*, 43 (2), 2005, pp. 283-306.

Cornwell, D.J., *Mercy. A Restorative Philosophy*, Hook, Hampshire, UK: Waterside Press, 2014a.

Cornwell, D.J., Blad J.R. & Wright, M. (Eds.), *Civilising Criminal Justice. An International Restorative Agenda for Penal Reform*, Hook, Hampshire, UK: Waterside Press, 2013.

Nussbaum, M., 'Equity and Mercy', in *Philosophy and Public Affairs* 22, 2, 1993 [Reprinted in J. Murphy (Ed.), *Punishment and Rehabilitation*, Belmont: Wadsworth, 1995, pp. 212-248].

Putnam, R., *Making Democracy Work*, Princeton, NJ: Princeton University Press, 1993.

Ronel, N. and Segev, D., *Positive Criminology*, New York and London: Routledge, 2015.

Schuilenberg, M.R., van Steden, R. & Oude Breuil, R. (Eds.), *Positive Criminology: Reflections on Care, Belonging and Security*. The Hague: Eleven International Publishing, 2014.

Walgrave, L., *Restorative Justice, Self-interest and Responsible Citizenship*, Cullompton, Devon, UK: Willan Publishing, 2008.

Wright, M. (1992), 'Victim-Offender Mediation as a Step Towards a Restorative System of Justice' in H. Messmer & H.U. Otto (Eds.), *Restorative Justice on Trial: Pitfalls and Potentials of Victim-Offender Mediation*, Dordrecht/Boston: Kluwer Academic Publishers, 1992, pp. 525-539.

Zehr, H., *The Little Book of Restorative Justice*, Intercourse (PA): Good Books, 2002.

Introduction

The concept of desert within a criminal justice context is, upon close examination, of a distinctly equivocal nature. Within the philosophy of criminal punishment in particular it has, over recent decades, become inextricably bound up with retributive notions of justice to the virtual exclusion of alternative explanations of its purpose. Desert is, in the commonly accepted interpretation of justice, 'what you get for what you did'. How much you get and in what form are thus issues of a subsidiary but directly associated nature. How the extent of desert is determined as the response to criminal acts is an altogether different matter and one certainly open to question.

This book is about the concept of desert, but in a much wider context than that of a retributive nature. It has been written because the penal process of England and Wales, like that of a number of other Western-style democracies, is locked into a state of political and operational stagnation, and lurches from crisis to crisis largely of its own making, from which only a determined programme of significant reform can make it 'fit for purpose'. Penal reform is almost always a politically unwelcome enterprise, frequently avoided or deferred because it threatens the electoral credibility of politicians and governments anxious to be perceived as 'tough on crime'. It also concerns directly the lives of that particular segment of every society that offends against its laws and is therefore deemed to be the least deserving of consideration when other social welfare priorities place pressure on limited national resources.

It is a book which should, therefore, concern politicians, policymakers, academics, students and researchers within the social sciences, criminal justice practitioners, penal reformers and informed members of the public alike. It has been prepared in as 'readable' a form as possible that is consistent with the complexity of the discussion within its inevitably wide-ranging debates and prescriptions for reform.

Penal processes and their administration are sometimes described as 'systems', a term which, in the case of that in England and Wales, is largely a misnomer. Even with the creation of a Ministry of Justice since 2007, there is little that could be described as 'systematic' about the manner in which justice is administered within its agencies, each with its own self-justifying remit, and with a scant sense of common purpose beyond that of allegiance to its own political masters. The term 'penal process' has been preferred and used throughout this work since it more accurately reflects the distinctly unsystematic manner in which justice within England and Wales is dispensed, as this work will testify.

Penal process reform, therefore, when it becomes necessary, has to be attempted against a backdrop of diverse and frequently exclusive political and inter-governmental interests, the activities of which are increasingly constrained by the need to compete for their share of scarce fiscal and other resources, and the more inward-looking as a result. This, in turn, makes consensus over the necessity for significant reform more difficult to achieve, however urgently that reform is needed.

The agencies that deliver the services necessary to deal with offenders on a day-to-day basis in either a custodial or a non-custodial form comprise, in the main, prisons and similar secure residential establishments and community-based correctional services. These can and should be 'systematically' organised, and the case for their being so on a unified basis is a strong one since their professional roles frequently overlap in dealing with offenders. In England and Wales both the Prison Service and National Probation Service (and to a lesser extent the Youth Justice Board) are agencies under the umbrella of the Ministry of Justice, and the former two fall within the operational control of its principal component, the National Offender Management Service (NOMS).[1] Much more will be noted about this arrangement within this work. The Prison Service is also responsible for the oversight and management of Immigration Removal Centres (IRCs), although the departmental responsibility for immigration and border security matters rests with the Home Office, which is also responsible for policing.

These structural issues and anomalies apart, and there are a number of others which will become evident later, the primary concern of this book is that of whether the criminal (and civil) justice process delivers to all of its legitimate stakeholders the quality of justice that they may reasonably expect and deserve.[2] Such an apparently straightforward question gives rise to a number of subsidiary ones that require some clarification in introducing this work which focuses predominantly upon criminal law issues and outcomes.

Perhaps the principal question that has to be answered is this. When criminal offences are committed, where does the focus of harm lie? Traditional explanations within the Anglo-Saxon concept of law insist that it is the state and its law that are transgressed since the law has been broken, the social order has been disturbed, and the transgression is therefore punishable. To whatever extent harm is occasioned thereby then becomes a matter of gravity (seriousness) and culpability (blameworthiness), and the penalty a matter of relative severity. Who or what has been harmed is thus a secondary or subsidiary issue.

1 The Youth Justice Board (YJB) which deals with juvenile offenders is an exception in this respect insofar as it is an executive non-departmental public body created by the Crime and Disorder Act 1998. Its twelve members are appointed by the Justice Secretary, and it operates in conjunction with the Ministry of Justice, the Department for Children, Schools and Families (DCSF), and to an extent still with the Home Office which was its former sponsor pre-2007. For a further explanation of the YJB and its operation, see: Gibson, 2009: 180-181.

2 Here it has to be noted that within the Anglo-Saxon tradition of justice a distinction is made between issues pertaining to individual rights and personal matters (and claims thereto) and wrongs or torts, and criminal matters which are the prerogative of the Crown. Thus civil courts and their proceedings deal with the former, while the criminal courts (Magistrates' and Crown Courts) deal with the latter. The two court systems differ in the standards of proof required for conviction, and in the manner of their proceedings and means of redress.

Alternative explanations within the more ancient cultures that predated the establishment of monarchical law predominantly during the Thirteenth Century in Europe would answer the same question differently. Here it would be insisted that someone or some persons have suffered the harm directly, and it is to them or to those affected that the redress is both due and deserved. The law, within such an understanding of justice, is merely a means by which offences are defined, and therefore cannot suffer the harm directly. Punishment (or sanction) may be due and appropriate, but it should – insofar as is possible – be used to make good or repair the harm done to those who have suffered it.[3]

The nature of desert within criminal justice hinges to a considerable, though not an absolute, extent upon this important debate as will become apparent within this book. An entitlement to redress, as we shall see, gives rise to desert claims which to an extent bridge the divide between civil and criminal law as it is presently perceived. The title of this work: *Desert in a Reparative Frame* thus provides the basis of the analysis within its pages.

There are, however, other and intriguing questions that remain to be answered. These concern the nature and appropriateness of the criminal justice process as it presently operates; who the legitimate stakeholders in criminal justice actually are; what all those who become involved in the process deserve from its delivery; and how this delivery could best be improved to the benefit of societies as a whole. These are important and, indeed, now urgent matters that extend far beyond the narrow confines of political manoeuvring and traditionalist myopia. The criminal justice process of England and Wales and certain other countries also stands at a crossroads: a redefinition of desert and its purposes might prove to be both the basis for long-overdue penal reform and the delivery of better justice in the future to all of its stakeholders. That is what this work sets out to achieve.

The structure of this book will be evident from the detailed list of contents which has preceded this introduction. From this it will be evident that the opening chapters (1 to 5) of Part 1 are devoted to an explanation of why the present state of criminal justice in England and Wales has reached a critical state as an outcome of its history and development, the philosophical implications of this development, and the reasons why significant strategic change has become urgently necessary. The remaining chapters (6 to 11) in Part 2 explain how a reconception of desert provides the basis for reform, the operational implications involved, and how these might be approached. The work is completed (in Chapter 12) with a summary of the main strands of discussion in the foregoing chapters, and a comprehensive bibliography and index.

The historical and philosophical perspectives of the development of the present *malaise* are essential to an understanding of why penal reform has become so necessary for countries

3 Such explanations are still to be found in the traditions and cultures of the 'first nations' peoples of North America, Africa, Australasia and some Middle Eastern countries. These have also been adopted by the proponents of the restorative justice movement worldwide since the 1970s and onwards.

having to live within strictly limited fiscal conditions and resources while retaining unacceptably high penal incarceration levels. These perspectives also indicate why previous attempts to reform have failed and have thus contributed to the contemporary situation. The prospective proposals are based upon providing 'better justice' to all the stakeholders legitimately affected by criminal offending – the state, communities, victims and offenders – through repairing harm, reducing crime and recidivism and, 'rendering to each what they actually deserve' from the criminal justice process. It is a book with a purpose, and the reader will decide whether this purpose has been achieved.

Part 1
Desert and Its Philosophical Implications

1 Towards De-Mystification

Background

From the earliest times of writings in the study of penology, the concept of desert has attracted the attention of philosophers in its relationship with the supposed justifications of 'criminal' punishment. In the overwhelming number of such instances, it became almost inseparably linked with the principle of retribution for wrongdoing in a retrospective sense that became accepted as axiomatic or logically self-evident in its essential 'rightness'. Wrongdoing, it was therefore proposed, required a response that was reciprocally punitive, visiting pain or at the least unpleasantness upon the perpetrator as a means of signalling both moral and social disapprobation of the offence and the offender.[1]

This much stated, it is also evident as Andrew von Hirsch (1976) has indicated, that the literature of penology of the Twentieth Century (and, indeed, of this new millennium) has paid little attention to the concept of desert beyond its seemingly inseparable link with retributive responses to crime within the philosophical literature (Id., 1976: 45-6).[2] My purpose in this work is to question this apparent inseparability, and to suggest that previous neglect of the desirability of doing so has led almost inevitably to a number of the deep-seated symptoms of the contemporary *malaise* that has engulfed many of the Western-style penal systems of the post-Modern era. The underlying urgency for such an inquiry may be seen to arise from concern that the taken-for-granted relationship between retribution and desert confines penal policymaking and judicial practices within a predominantly retrospective and increasingly punitive mode of justice administration which is, in fact, significantly counter-productive in relation to crime reduction.[3] Such a mode of behaviour as the preferred response to crime may have some presumptive resonance for assumptions in relation to crime control, but as will become apparent later, it is altogether

1 Here, it will be noted that the term 'criminal' punishment has been used in a general sense of wrongdoing within the context of the criminal law. Such offences may also be determined and sanctioned in the civil (or other non-criminal) courts, including those of an ecclesiastical or similar nature.

2 See also, in particular, his introductory footnote to the Notes to Chapter 6 on p. 160, though it will be evident that many offences constitute civil torts or wrongs that may not fall within the jurisdiction of the criminal law.

3 In England and Wales for example, and insofar as imprisonment is concerned, most recently published criminal justice statistics indicate that 46.9% of all imprisoned adults are reconvicted within 12 months of release. For those serving sentences of less than 12 months, this rate rises to 58.3%, and for those who have served eleven or more previous custodial sentences the rate rises to 68.9% (Ministry of Justice, Proven Re-offending Quarterly – October 2010 to September 2011, Tables 18a, 19a and 7a, London: Ministry of Justice, 2013a).

questionable whether that particular endeavour amounts to much more than a political pipedream.

This work is predicated on the premise that crime reduction should and can be a prospective enterprise for pro-active rather than reactive criminal justice processes. Indeed, the penological stalemate engendered by predominantly retrospective responses to crime may be said to lead directly to forms of penal instrumentalism[4] in which offenders are used as means rather than ends in pursuit of crime control – and that this, in itself, is morally questionable.

If crime reduction is to be perceived as the principal purpose of justice administration, then the means have to be found of persuading offenders not only of the moral 'wrongness' and harmfulness of their behaviour, but also that a law-abiding lifestyle is preferable to that of continuing criminality. It is also a matter of statistical record[5] that the lives of many offenders are significantly affected by social deficits[6] that place limitations on their social functioning and reduce their resistance to the temptation to offend. Moreover, when such persons do commit offences, dealing with them in a predominantly retributive manner does little, if anything, to overcome such deficits and may all too easily compound their problems.

Such is not to suggest that offending should not have consequences for the offender, but rather that these consequences should be constructive rather than destructive in terms of outcomes. It will be seen to be a matter of pivotal debate within this work whether retributive modes of criminal justice administration, focused predominantly upon punishing offences retrospectively, are more or less likely than prospective and reparative alternative strategies to promote attitudinal and behavioural change within the majority of all but the most serious of offenders. This debate necessarily brings into question, and centrally addresses, the essential nature of criminal desert which has for too long mystified and even confused both the literature and the practices of criminal punishment.

It is, of course, undeniably the case that the link between retribution and desert has dominated the discourses of criminal punishment since as far back as historical accounts of justice can be traced. Indeed, it can be claimed – as we shall see in Chapter 2 – that desert has, to a marked extent, come to be seen as the legitimising justification for retributive behavioural responses to crime as a means of demonstrating the necessity for

4 By which is meant the use of criminal punishment and offenders for the pursuit of social policy objectives beyond the strictly necessary response to offending. Here see my detailed explanation in Cornwell (2007: 24-27 and *passim*), and Blad (2006: 137).

5 See here for example, the excellent statistical explanations available in documentary form provided by organisations such as the Prison Reform Trust in its periodic Bromley Briefings on the UK criminal justice system (Prison Reform Trust, 2014).

6 Such as lower than average levels of educational achievement, family and relationship breakdown, environmental poverty, physical and/or mental health issues, substance addiction, homelessness, lack of regular employment, and the like.

law enforcement, and that the law 'has teeth that bite'. This much conceded, however, the term 'desert' as defined in most reliable dictionaries is open to other avenues of interpretation. One such is the concept of desert as 'something merited' as a matter of justice or fairness, though without any necessary connotation of retributive reciprocity. We shall return to this notion in subsequent discussion within this work.

As the title of this chapter suggests, the practice of criminal punishment has, over time, developed a mystique heavily invested with philosophical underpinnings and explanations rooted in the academic discourses, disputations and conversations of the post-Enlightenment Period and onwards to the present day. The academic discipline of criminology as the study of crime, of its causes, and of attempts to control and prevent it (penology) has developed and expanded during the post-World War II years of the Twentieth Century in particular, drawing heavily upon the work and approaches of the related disciplines of philosophy, ethics, theology, sociology, law and jurisprudence, and of medical science, psychiatry and psychology. The hybrid nature of this development, while widening the nature of criminological discourse, has also served to oblige criminologists to be aware of and acknowledge these developments within their own research programmes and policy considerations.

Justifying Criminal Punishment – A Brief Historical Overview

The formative explanations of the justifications of criminal punishment found in the works of Beccaria (1764), Bentham (1780/1789), Kant (1797), Hegel (1821), Mill (1863), Bradley (1876), Green (1881), Bosanquet (1899) and others were further developed most notably during the early Twentieth Century by Rashdall (1907/1924), Ewing (1929/1963)), Ross (1930), and Mabbott (1939/1955) in the pre-World War II era. During the post-War period up to 1970, a further group of influential academic writers – most of whom were philosophers – continued this work with a renewed energy, as may be seen in the contributions of Quinton, Flew, Mundle, Rawls, Benn, and Armstrong – all reproduced in Acton (1969) – and of Hart (1962/1968), Feinberg (1962/1965) and Honderich (1976).

The immediate post-World War II era in Western Europe was characterised by the emergence of the 'rehabilitative ideal' in penal practices, predicated on the belief that the key to reducing crime and recidivism lay in promoting behavioural change in offenders through 'treatment and training' to assist them in leading 'good and useful lives'. The concept, however well intentioned, resulted in a burgeoning of therapeutic initiatives and training programmes, heavily overlaid by a '*quasi*-medical' approach delivered by a new generation of correctional professionals trained in social work, probation practice, clinical psychology and psychiatric medical intervention.

If the model had a measurable impact, it lay predominantly in an increase in the use of indeterminate sentences and also of administrative discretion[7] which led, through extended duration of sentences, to a rapid and sustained increase in penal populations. To make matters worse, crime rates and recidivism showed no measurable signs of reduction, and disenchantment with the rehabilitative ideal became widespread. Its eventual abandonment was accelerated by the publication in the USA and Britain of a study conducted in the early 1970s into the effectiveness of correctional treatment programmes (Lipton, Martinson & Wilks, 1975) which concluded that no particular forms of intervention were any more successful than any others, and which had been preceded by an article in *The Public Interest* 1974 (Spring) by Martinson of an even more negative nature (Martinson, 1974). The rehabilitative era eventually became known as the 'Nothing Works' era as a result.

The 1970s proved to be watershed years in the further development of criminal punishment philosophy. With the eventual and inevitable demise of the rehabilitative ethic as the decade began,[8] and the publication in the USA of the Report of the American Friends Service Committee entitled *Struggle for Justice* in 1972, an entirely new model of corrections was proposed, and based on the concept of strictly proportionate punishment, of 'just deserts', of the limitation of judicial and administrative discretion, and of an end to sentencing indeterminacy.

The 'Justice Model' as it became known, was designed to 'plug the gap' or penological vacuum created by abandonment of the rehabilitative ethic without an inevitable return to increasingly punitive sentencing. Though the model as advanced by Andrew von Hirsch and others (von Hirsch, 1976) gained some support in the USA and Western Europe, it was not without its detractors and critics (*e.g.* Hudson, 1987, *passim*; Bottomley, 1979: 148-53; Bean, 1981: 172-4 among several). The result was that the model fell prey to the objections of judiciaries and penal administrators on the one hand, and politicians anxious to retain electoral credibility by being 'tough on crime' on the other. Somewhat inevitably, a return to primarily retributive and deterrent sentencing displaced it during the late 1980s, and remains in place in many Western-style democracies to this day.

---

7 Vested in the power of prison officials and parole authorities to delay or withhold release of prisoners on grounds of showing no measurable improvement in behavioural terms, or failing to respond positively to the various forms of therapeutic, medical or training initiatives put into operation.

8 For an explanation of how this occurred see my analysis in Cornwell (2006: 31-32 and *passim*), and Hudson (1987: 29-30 *et seq.*).

'BLEAK HOUSE' – THE FUTURE OF PUNISHMENT JUSTIFICATIONS

The pendulum swings of criminal punishment philosophy described – albeit briefly – in the foregoing account must, to many observers of criminal justice, seem mystifying in the extreme. From pre-World War II emphasis on retribution and deterrence to post-War rehabilitationism, and from thence to the 'Justice Model' and subsequently a return to retribution and incapacitation presents a cyclic picture of a despairing enterprise.

In a wide-ranging and perceptive work published as the new millennium began, David Garland (2002) chronicled the social, economic and structural changes that have taken place in Britain and the USA during the latter half of the Twentieth Century. He has also indicated with admirable clarity the 'transformation of criminological thought' that has accompanied these changes (2002: 15-26):

> In the period since the 1970s, a quite different set of criminological ideas has begun to emerge and to influence government policy. The theories that now shape official thinking and action are *control theories* of various kinds that deem crime and delinquency to be problems not of deprivation but of inadequate controls. Social controls, situational controls, self-controls – these are the now-dominant themes of contemporary criminology and of the crime control policies to which they give rise. (Garland, 2002: 15) [Italics in original]

Such an analysis goes a considerable way to explaining the expansion of 'managerialism' within the criminal justice arena that occurred during the 1990s and onwards, combined with a significant increase in legislative provisions designed to 'control' anti-social behaviour in pursuit of social protection by means of increasing use of incapacitation of offenders to pre-empt further offending. Punishment of increasing severity could be justified not predominantly on the basis of desert, but rather as a means of retribution and a misplaced, though still persistent espousal of the deterrence theory.

This new *genre* of instrumentalism confounds the previously supposed purposes of criminal punishment by deliberately selecting out various forms of offending and offender for exemplary penalties. This is done in pursuit of social policy objectives ostensibly designed to allay the perceived public fear of victimisation prompted to a considerable extent by sensational treatment of such crime in the mass media.[9] This leads in turn to the

9 Most notably violent and sexual offenders considered likely to re-offend similarly, and whose detention on an indeterminate basis can be justified as in the public interest. Here it should be noted, however, that the latest Crime Survey Statistics for England and Wales 2011/12 indicate a continuing downward trend in serious violent and sexual offences recorded by the police, and in rates of victimisation. The likelihood of the average citizen becoming a victim of such crime has reduced by almost 50% between 1996 and 2011 (Office for National Statistics, 2012: tables various for key offences). The same trends are also evident in the

danger of a situation in which laws are made to deal disproportionally with specific forms of offending for the overriding purpose of controlling crime primarily on the basis of individual and general deterrence, the effectiveness of which is altogether unknowable. In so doing it also distorts the retributive purpose of punishment to levels beyond that which could be considered strictly deserved.

All of this, if my foregoing analysis is close to the reality of both moral and contemporary criminal punishment purposes, leaves criminal justice in a state of operational turmoil and uncertainty. For although the principles of punishment revealed in the criminological literature of its formative period – and held also to be the justifications for the practices of punishment – were considered to be sustainable in moral argument,[10] the operational use to which these have been put in the contemporary approaches to justice administration have become morally and ethically questionable.

It is also of interest to note that, since the late 1990s, very few books of a substantive nature have been written about criminal punishment. This fact may suggest either that the entire nature of the debate has become so diffuse and equivocal as to make the relationships between its constituent and supposed principles or justifications incoherently mystifying. Or perhaps, that all that could be said has already been said, and that further conversations are merely repetitious and largely unhelpful. As will be evident from this work, I do not subscribe to such a view.

The Need for This Work

Why, then, a book focusing on desert as a justification of punishment at this time? As a means of providing a platform of explanation for the chapters that follow, I offer the following illustrative explanation. The criminal justice landscape within many Western-style democracies has come to resemble a jig-saw puzzle, the pieces of which should, in theory, mesh together to form a consistent image or picture that is recognisable and meaningful to the onlooker.[11]

crime statistics of the majority of the Western European countries, see: Council of Europe, 2013: Tables 1-8.

10 Even though, as the same literature demonstrates very clearly, there were evident differences of analytical opinion and approach between moral philosophers as to what did or did not amount to 'cardinal justifications' and the relationships between the generally accepted principles. Here, see in particular, the contributions in H.B. Acton (1969) as an excellent example.

11 By the term 'onlooker' used here I imply any person seeking to complete the puzzle by locating the constituent pieces together to form a coherent image. In criminal justice terms such persons might be academics, students of criminology, legal, judicial or correctional practitioners, penal policymakers, politicians, or even inquiring members of the public.

Upon opening the box to assemble the pieces of this puzzle, it becomes evident that the borders are of an irregular nature rather than straight, and that pieces which should logically fit together within its interior design fail to do so, even though each is readily identifiable. The result is a confusing jumble of images each of which appears to have some relevance for the whole, but whose edges appear to defy assembly into a coherent design.

How, then, can sense be made of such a situation? One way might be to turn all the pieces upside down, assemble them without an overall design until all are in place, and then reverse the whole and identify where the apparent mismatches and inconsistencies have occurred. Another might be to leave the pieces the right way up and, ignoring the supposed design, fit the matching ones together until all are in place and see what results. Either way, a number of the pieces may have to be redesigned or re-arranged to make the overall picture consistent and understandable.

Such a situation is, it might be suggested, illustrative of the present circumstances in which the image of criminal justice exists, and in which also the debate in relation to the justifications, principles or purposes of punishment has become stranded. Some of the pieces of the puzzle must, evidently, occupy the central area of the design; others may be of a more tangential nature, but nevertheless fulfil a peripheral purpose in making the picture complete. Until a clear design becomes apparent, however, it will remain impossible to suggest what extent of re-arrangement might remedy the situation.

To many 'onlookers' who may have some understanding of the structure of criminal justice it will be evident that, in relation to criminal punishment, the centre ground of the puzzle must contain images of retribution, deterrence, incapacitation, reparation and rehabilitation (or restoration) as *purposes* of punishment at the least. These pieces are, in turn, dependent upon notions such as fairness (or impartiality), equity, equality, propriety, desert and legality, each of which are attributes of justice itself and impact upon the *practices* of punishment. More remotely, perhaps, lie a number of procedural considerations relating to justice administration such as due process, culpability, mitigation, aggravation, mercy and discretion, which affect the *quality* of justice delivery.

And, lest they be overlooked, there is also an extensive list of the *dramatis personae* of criminal justice which includes (in some sort of order of appearance) academics, policy-makers, politicians, offenders, victims, police and prosecution authorities, judiciaries, legal professionals, correctional officials, dependents and communities all of whom, in different roles, become involved in the justice process. To each of these constituencies the operation of criminal justice has to make reasonable sense because otherwise it becomes disreputable.

Now, it may be contended that making sense of the *purposes* of criminal punishment must be the starting point for meaningful assembly of the puzzle. However, the purposes do not stand alone without consideration of the *practices* which must be consistent with the principles (or justifications) that underpin the purposes.[12] Without this relationship being one of congruence, the *quality* of justice administration and its delivery cannot be assured, and the entire focus of the assembly becomes blurred and incoherent. Such, indeed, is the case as Ted Honderich has argued, where bad laws are enacted and punishment for breaking them would be entirely unjustified (Honderich, 1976: 24). Thus if there is an obligation that amounts to a justification of punishment, then it resides in the actual morality of the law, rather than in the fact that a law merely exists (Cornwell, 2006: 43).

If we were to accept that the supposed purposes of criminal punishment are confined to retribution, deterrence, incapacitation, reparation and restoration (or rehabilitation) alone, but possibly in some forms of combination, and that the principles governing the imposition of such punishment are as Hart proposed them (and accepting Honderich's objection), does the image of the puzzle achieve a clearer focus? Sadly, it has to be suggested that it does not.

The reasons that I wish to advance for this contention are essentially twofold: the first is that I believe that Hart's cardinal principles were actually incomplete in an essential dimension; and the second is that this omission critically affects the morality of any justification of punishment. Now, had Hart insisted that punishment *per se* had to be deserved, and that without desert the morality of punishment would be unjustifiable – whatever its purposes – then this crucial difficulty would never have arisen.

Such a contention, if accepted, would place the concept of desert at the centre of criminal punishment considerations, and as a result, add a much needed and hitherto largely neglected evaluative dimension in relation to future conversations concerning the morality of the perceived purposes of punishment itself. It is towards achieving this 'shift' in the literature and practices of penology, and to discussion of the consequent implications, that the remaining chapters of this work are devoted.

In Chapter 2, we trace the origins of the notion of desert from the earliest recorded writings in penology to the present day. In so doing, it will become apparent that, although the notion may have been implicitly present in the earliest formulations of legal codes, it was not explicitly recognised in traceable form until the era of the Roman Empire during the later centuries BC. Thereafter, desert became almost inseparably associated with retributive punishment in a largely unrefined and taken-for-granted state until the Enlightenment Period of the Eighteenth Century in Europe.

12 There has, in some of the literature on criminal punishment, been an evident tendency to treat the principles and purposes as interchangeable notions. I suggest here that do so adds an unnecessary confusion to such explanations. My preference is to establish that the principles identified as the 'standard case of punishment' by H.L.A. Hart (1968: 4-5) remain a guiding, though questionably incomplete definitional text. In summary, Hart insisted that punishment must involve unpleasantness, be for an offence against legal rules, and be of an actual or supposed offender for such an offence. It must also be intentionally administered by human beings acting for an authority constituted by a legal system against which the offence was committed and proven.

2 Whence the Concept of Desert?

Pre-Enlightenment Thinking

As we have noted in Chapter 1, the concept of desert has been implicitly present within the criminological literature for centuries past, though generally it was presented as a justifying aspect of retributive punishment. This fact is demonstrable from study of the ancient legal codes of the Middle East, the Mediterranean and the Chinese dynasties which variously appeared between 2,380 BC and the early centuries AD.[1] Of these codes, that of Hammurabi King of Babylon is perhaps the finest example, consisting as it did in the specification of 282 laws that included both criminal and civil offences with penalties for infraction cited, and which also included specific provision for reparation in default in certain instances.[2]

The works of the Greek philosopher Plato (428-348 BC) emphasised the social basis of justice as a means of ordering human affairs by fostering positive relationships between citizens in a collective sense. This ordering ensured harmony, limited individualism and an emphasis on personal rights.[3] Somewhat later, and following in the same Greek philosophical tradition, Aristotle (384-322 BC) proposed that 'natural and universal justice' should form the basis of laws, rather than state-dictated justice which was particularly limited to the needs of governments, and therefore of an inferior quality.[4]

Though these early codes and philosophical writings did not specify the concept of desert directly in circumstances in which penalties are prescribed, mention of it does appear in the writings of Lucius Seneca (*circa* 4BC-65 AD) the Roman Stoic philosopher and statesman in an essay written to the Emperor Nero which includes the following statement: 'Everybody, however, understands that the fact of the case is that mercy consists in stopping short of what might have been deservedly proposed' (Seneca, *circa* 300 AD).The Roman concept of justice did, however, differ markedly in approach from that of the Greek, its predecessor. Here, the emphasis changed to perceive law as 'an aggregation of personal

1 These codes (sometimes known as codexes) included those notably of Urukagina (2,380-2,360 BC), Ur-Nammu (*circa* 2,350 BC), Hammurabi (*circa* 1,790 BC), Nesilim/Eshnunna (*circa* 1,650 BC), the Mosaic Law/Torah (9th to 5th centuries BC), the *Corpus Juris Civilis* or Justinian Code (529-534 BC), The Twelve Tables of Roman Law (451 BC), Sharia/Islamic Law (*circa* 570 AD), the Tang Code (624-637 AD), and the Jewish religious law (Halakha), later incorporating Talmudic and Rabbinical law and customs evolved from dates uncertain BC. For a full description see: http://en.wikipedia.org/wik/List_of_ancient_legal_codes (Accessed 7 November 2014).

2 See: https://en.wikipedia.org/Code_of_Hammurabi (Accessed 10 November 2014).

3 Most notably in 'Laws', in Plato, 1997a, and in 'Republic', Plato, 1997b.

4 Here see: Aristotle, The Nicomachean Ethics, 2nd ed., [Tr. T. Irwin], Indianapolis: Hackett, 1999, and for a more detailed explanation: E. Younkins, 'Justice in a Free Society', Quebec: Liberty Free Press, 2000, (March), p. 1. Also at: www.quebecoislibre.org/younkins27.htm (Accessed 21 November 2014).

rights' designed to give every person his rights, and justice administration became formalised as a legal function of the state, rather than as the social concern of all citizens (Younkins, 2000: 1-2).

The development of Roman law, with its emphasis on preserving equality of rights between individuals, implied that every law-abiding citizen should receive rewards appropriate to his work or social contribution, and thus the concept of freedom and responsibility in his dealings with others. It was, in effect, the *naissance* of what has come to be known as 'commutative' justice, and which ultimately passed into European legal codes, and into English and American law (Younkins, Id.).

This brief explanation of the earliest origins of legal codes and ideas would be incomplete without mention of the emergence of ecclesiastic law[5] derived from the works most notably of Saint Augustine (354-430 AD) and of Saint Thomas Aquinas (1225-1274). Augustine is regarded by many scholars as the first Western philosopher, the legacy of whose writings extended into and beyond the post-Enlightenment Period of European ecclesiastical and political thought in relation to the administration of justice based upon 'natural law' rather than state-imposed jurisprudence based upon 'giving every man his due'.[6]

Thomas Aquinas, following Augustine, and also in the Aristotelian tradition of sophistry, is noted particularly for his *Summa Theologiae* written between 1265 and 1274 and unfinished due to his death, in which he specifically addressed questions of law (Q90) and the essential nature of law (Q91) within emerging Western societies.[7]

Through the centuries thereafter, and until the Enlightenment Period of the Eighteenth Century and onwards, desert remained firmly linked to retributive punishment in relation to both criminal and civil offences. It seems, therefore, to have been axiomatically evident, and accepted beyond apparent questioning, that crimes (and other social wrongs) required a punitive response to preserve the authority of state law, and that whatever form of retributive penalty was prescribed was morally acceptable because the offender – as a matter of culpability – had brought the punishment upon himself, and it was therefore deserved.

During this period, the works of Thomas Hobbes (1588-1679) and John Locke (1632-1704) emerged to question once again the nature of laws and the legitimate means of administering justice. Hobbes acknowledged the existence of both an 'immortal God' and a 'mortal God' (the State) which he called the Leviathan (Hobbes, 1651). He maintained that the state was the custodian of both secular and spiritual power, and could therefore

5 A term derived from the word *ecclesia* (C.16: from medieval Latin and late Greek) meaning a congregation or assembly of citizens within the Greek state for the purpose of deciding issues of communal importance, and subsequently a religious gathering for worship within the Christian tradition.

6 See, *e.g.*: Augustine: 1956.

7 For a detailed explanation of Aquinas' work, see http://en.wikipedia.org/wk1/Summa_Theologiae (Accessed 22 November 2104).

create, confirm and take away rights. Justice, as Hobbes conceived it, was the exercise of state power in relation to wrongdoing, and was legitimised by the *de facto* existence of the state, though whether in the form of a democracy or monarchical authority remains somewhat unclear. Hobbes' preference was clearly for a sovereign state with a monarch to whom, in the form of a social contract, citizens surrendered part of their individual rights towards the common wellbeing. This ruler would have complete power, including that over religion, which placed Hobbes in a confrontational situation, and led to him being denounced by the religious leaders as a subversive and an atheist. Such was their power within the society of the time that the ecclesiastical hierarchy ultimately stopped Hobbes from publishing his works, in spite of his being admired and befriended by King Charles II (Greene, 1967: 209-215).

Though his work may have had limited immediate impact, it had a much greater influence on the subsequent development of political and legal thought during the years of the Enlightenment and thereafter than this brief *résumé* can do justice to. He firmly established the sovereignty of the nation-state, and that its power and the authority of the law are justified 'only because they contribute to the security of individual human beings, and that there is no sensible ground of obedience and respect for authority except the anticipation that these will yield a larger individual advantage than would their absence' (Id: 215).[8]

John Locke (1632-1704) was both an economist and a philosopher devoted to the development of democratic as opposed to feudal government, and to expanding the influence of natural law and religious toleration. When the 'Glorious Revolution' of 1688 brought William of Orange to the English throne as a means of preventing the accession of a Catholic king, monarchical power was transferred from the sovereign to Parliament: a transition which was expressly designed to provide for the maintenance of individual liberties and encourage the spirit of free scientific inquiry. Locke's natural law was based upon a form of the social contract similar to that advocated by Hobbes, the consent of the governed, and insistence that no man or government has the arbitrary power over the life, liberty or possessions of another (Id: 237).[9]

THE ENLIGHTENMENT ERA AND ONWARDS

It is in the works of Hobbes and Locke that we may perceive the *naissance* of the development of the concept of laws that, among other philosophical interpretations of utilitarian

8 For a comprehensive commentary on Hobbes and his contribution to subsequent and contemporary political thought see: Armitage, 2007; and Finkelstein, 2005.

9 A sentiment subsequently adopted by Thomas Jefferson in drafting the American Declaration of Independence in 1776, and which remains enshrined in the American Constitution to the present day.

social contract theory and the sovereign state, prevailed during the Enlightenment Era in which Jeremy Bentham and later Henry Sidgwick came to particular prominence within penology.

Accounts of the life and beliefs of Jeremy Bentham (1748-1832) differ considerably depending upon the approaches adopted by those commentators that have compiled them. Clearly he was a complex and socially aware person, Oxford educated from the age of twelve years, probably an agnostic, and a man with a deep interest in the functioning of the society in which he lived and worked. He was a qualified lawyer, to an extent eccentric in his views, a utilitarian by conviction, and devoted to the interpretation of such principles in public affairs. Curiously, according to Greene (1967: 309-313), he was 'a democrat in the sense of believing that government ought to act in the interest of the people, but he was not a democrat in the sense of believing that government ought to be carried out by the people. He also had a deep distrust of the English legal system, the procedures of which he perceived as 'a collection of superstitions, fallacies, confusions and devices to enrich lawyers and judicial officers at the expense of those who came before the bar of justice' (Id: 309-310).

Whether Bentham was in fact a reformer or rather a great theorist of reform remains an open question. He was a trenchant critic of existing institutions[10] and government practices in which he perceived the need for reform, but was frustrated by the resistance to reform which he encountered in his dealings with government officials, politicians and legal practitioners. Widely travelled in Europe and elsewhere, Bentham saw structural reform of prisons as an urgent social necessity to relieve deplorable, brutal, insanitary and degrading conditions, and also to outlaw the prevailing culture of corruption and other forms of malpractice evident in the dealings of prison officials with their charges (Ignatieff, 1978: 74-5 and *passim*).

He was, however, clearly ambivalent about the root causes of criminality and its treatment, at times regarding prisoners as incorrigibles beyond the hope of reform or salvation, and at other times as victims of disadvantage in need of socialisation, encouragement and the inculcation of discipline in their lives. His adoption of the American panopticon penitentiary design for a new generation of English prisons was as much a deliberate means of making the working practices of prison staff more visible as it was of improving the conditions of prisoners and making control and employment of them more efficiently managed.[11]

Perhaps the most significant aspect of Bentham's contribution to the penology of his period was, in fact, an unstated but nevertheless implicitly evident conviction that the

10 And, in particular, of the principles, practices and conditions of the English penal system, toward the reform of which he devoted a major part of his active life.

11 For a detailed account of these developments see: Ignatieff, 1978, in Chapters Three and Four, pages 44-113.

conditions in which criminals were held in state custody were not merely undeserved, but that such conditions also infringed the accepted principles of morality and probity.[12] It was, however, the inefficiency of the penal process in reforming criminals as perceived by Bentham that prompted his reformist motivations. These same sentiments were later to emerge in the work of one of his most noted utilitarian disciples, John Stuart Mill.

J.S. Mill (1806-1873) was well known to Bentham who was a friend and colleague of his father, James Mill, both being members of the reform group known as the 'philosophical radicals' and of which Bentham was the intellectual leader. The group later became known as Utilitarians. Mill deserves brief mention here, not because of his contribution to penology, but rather because of his similar approach to government reform as a member of parliament (albeit briefly between 1865 and 1868) and his reputation as an economist and liberal thinker.

The sheer volume and width of Mill's writings was truly monumental, as was made evident in his *Collected Works* edited by John Robson, and comprising thirty-three volumes assembled and edited between 1965 and 1991 and published by the University of Toronto Press.[13] Though Mill was not without his critics, mainly among the 'establishment' figures of the era and those reluctant to support programmes of significant economic and political reform,[14] his far-sightedness made him a thinker and philosopher far ahead of his times and, ultimately after his death, the economist whose ideas became the basis of English Fabian socialism (Greene, 1967: 383-4).

The reader of this work so far may be surprised at the apparent absence of references to desert in all but a few of the many works cited. The reason for this absence lies, in my estimation, in the simple fact that until the end of the Enlightenment Era and even for some time thereafter the practices of retributive justice retained a primacy in which desert was the axiomatic and taken-for-granted justification for the infliction of punishment – frequently of a brutal and painful nature. In short, retributive punishment was seen as the logical and inescapable response to criminal acts, and was justified (or deserved) because the offender had 'brought the punishment upon himself'.

This situation changed with the writings of Henry Sidgwick (1838-1900), and in particular with the publication of his treatise *The Methods of Ethics* in 1893. Sidgwick was, by any standard, a remarkable man: a philosopher, politician, poet, sociologist and psychologist. He also had a deep interest in the paranormal. His working life was spent at Trinity College Cambridge as a student, fellow, and eventually as Knightsbridge Professor of Moral Phi-

12 A situation which seems to persist in the present era in which many prisons in England and Wales hold numbers of prisoners considerably in excess of the accommodation levels which they were originally designed to meet (See: Prison Reform Trust, 2013, on p. 2 of Chapter One, Note 5).

13 These works included *Utilitarianism, On Liberty, A System of Logic, and Principles of Political Economy*, and are clearly but concisely surveyed by Brink, 2014.

14 Including the much needed expansion of women's sufferage as has been indicated by J Urmson (1953: 33-39.

losophy from 1883 until the year of his death in 1900. He was also instrumental (with his wife) in the founding of Newnham College Cambridge in 1875, the first college for women in the university, and of which his wife Eleanor became principal in 1892.[15]

In dealing with the difficulties inherent in the concept of desert within criminal justice, Sidgwick refers to both Plato and Aristotle as the authorities subsequently incorporated and accepted within Christian theology in relation to punishment for wrongdoing and the requital by individuals of personal harms. However, he goes further:

> But in its universalised form the old conviction still lingers in the popular view of Criminal justice: it seems still to be widely held that Justice requires pain to be inflicted on a man who has done wrong, even if no benefit result either to him or to others from the pain. I hesitate to attribute (this) to Common Sense, since I think it is gradually passing away from the moral consciousness of educated persons in the most advanced communities: but I think it is still perhaps the more ordinary view. (Sidgwick, 1893: 18-19)[16]

Sidgwick made a clear distinction between corrective (or retributive) justice, compensatory justice and distributive justice, as subsequently have Velasquez, Andre, Shanks *et al.* (1990) and others such as Rawls (1971 and 2001). He was also at pains to indicate the difference between 'good desert' or merit and 'ill desert' as the traditional responses to criminal acts deliberately committed with wrong intention. As we shall see later, Honderich (1976) provides a more contemporary commentary on these matters.

During the closing years of the Nineteenth Century, a number of other philosophers writing within the tradition of the English-speaking world added to the debate concerning the justifications for, and purposes of, criminal punishment. Prominent among these commentators were, in order of their contributions, the idealists Francis Bradley (1876), Thomas Green (1881) and Bernard Bosanquet (1918). In summary, Bradley criticised, albeit in a somewhat limited manner, J.S. Mill's utilitarian contention that punishment was only justifiable as a means of benefiting the offender and protecting others (Acton, 1969: 1). Green advanced the view that punishment was justified primarily due to the offender's violation of the rights of others, and as a means of rectifying that situation. Bosanquet, like Green, saw punishment as axiomatically deserved, as a legitimate means of imposing retribution on offenders, and as a means of taking their actions seriously as deliberate acts.

15 For an expanded biography of Sidgwick's life see: www.henrysidgwick.com/biography.eng.html (Accessed 27 November 2014). See also: Schultz, 2012.

16 Reproduced from Chapter V of Book III of Sidgwick, 1893: 3-28.

Thus, as the century closed, the debate concerning criminal punishment had widened into a variety of explanations, even though the nature of desert remained largely confined to retributive predispositions focused on offenders and their offences, rather than focused upon the wider concepts of distributive and compensatory justice.

Into the Twentieth Century

During the first half of the century, attention began to turn in a different direction, primarily due to the work of three notably non-idealist or 'realist' critics of the punishment theories previously discussed. These critics were Hastings Rashdall (1891 and 1907/1924), A.C. Ewing (1929) and Sir David Ross (1930) respectively.

Rashdall was critical of the retributive theory of punishment and desert as proposed by Bradley *et al.*, and as previously mentioned, in three important respects: first, the impossibility of making punishment commensurable with moral guilt; second, even if the two were commensurable, that any addition to the punishment of pain for the purposes of deterrence or reform would be unjust; and third, that acceptance of the retributive view would imply that forgiveness was always wrong (Acton, 1969: 13). Thus, in Rashdall's estimation, all that remained in the retributive approach, once the moral objections had been exposed, was an insistence that punishment should only be imposed on the guilty – a fact that most reasonable persons would accept as evidently obvious.

A.C. Ewing accepted the non-commensurability argument of Rashdall in relation to retributive punishment, but was also of the view that neither reform nor deterrence could provide a morally defensible main justification for punishment (1929: 37-39 and *passim*). This evidently left him in some difficulty, since he also perceived desert as being an integral ingredient of the commensurability argument which, in default of the possibility of determining with accuracy its due and just extent, created even greater confusion. It seems strange, therefore, that in an exposition as detailed and closely argued as Ewing's, desert received no further substantive consideration until the closing part of the book in which it was discussed in relation to merit (1929: 126-128).

Sir David Ross, while accepting the difficulties of the commensurability argument, adopted an entirely different approach to the justification of punishment. This approach was based upon a view of crime as a violation of the rights of other (and presumably innocent) citizens, and that crime thus had to be punished in the public interest. Further, that the state had a right to injure any of its members in the public interest, but because the criminal has injured others, it has a special right to injure him. Moreover, in so doing, the state is keeping a promise which, in establishing the criminal law, it makes to any victim and to anyone in its jurisdiction (Acton, 1969: 14-15). It flows from this conception of justice that it is justifiable, in the public interest, to impose deterrent or reformatory punishment upon someone who has infringed the rights of others. Thus Ross extricated himself from accepting retributive justifications by means of the more generalised argument for a 'public interest' rationale.

The Punishment Debate in the Modern Era

Post-World War II there emerged a resurgent interest in the punishment debate throughout Western Europe, and in North America. In the United Kingdom, as has been indicated in Chapter 1, a number of leading academics – mainly in the disciplines of moral, ethical and legal philosophy – featured prominently in these conversations. A similar development was also occurring in North America and Northern Europe, particularly in the Scandinavian countries, and in the Netherlands and Belgium in which post-war reconstruction was taking place with a renewed emphasis on political freedom, international cooperation, and increasing social democracy.

In the 1950s and 1960s in the United Kingdom in particular, the punishment debate expanded – though very much in the same mould as that in which it has been set in the immediate pre-War era. Of the writers mentioned previously in this chapter and the one preceding it, only Mundle (1954) made an explicit attempt to deal with the difficulties evident in accommodating the concept of desert within and beyond retributive explanations of penology. In doing so, he tied himself to arguments based on proportionality which subsequently von Hirsch (1972 and 1976) and his associates foundered upon in justifying the 'Justice Model'. This model eventually failed to achieve acknowledged operational credibility (cf. Hudson, 1987; and earlier, Bottomley, 1979).

Elaborations of the 'commensurate deserts' concept articulated by von Hirsch *et al.* in the Justice Model, and also in particular by Feinberg (1970), gave rise to a considerable volume of journal (and other) literature in the United States during the 1970s and onwards (*cf. e.g.* Sher, 1987; Sterba, 1974 and 1976; Miller, 1976; McLeod, 1999; Smilansky, 2006). Interpretations of the model in its apparent applicability to other and wider aspects of social justice proliferated because as, Hudson has argued, the model 'appeared to offer all things to all people' (1987: 37-8).

This much stated, however, and within the criminal justice arena, little if anything seemed able to shift the notion of desert away from its retributive association with that of some sort of equivalence between penalty and offence (Honderich, 1976: 29-30). But there are problems with this apparently self-evident assertion:

> Sometimes people say that a man deserves something and intend that it is no more than right that he get it. To attempt to argue that a man's punishment is justified, by saying in this sense that deserves it, is obviously pointless. Any

> desert claim that reduces to the assertion that it is obligatory or permissible to impose a penalty cannot, of course, be offered as a reason for the proposition in dispute, that it is obligatory or permissible to impose the penalty. This is a simple fallacy where the supposed reason is identical with the supposed conclusion. It is a simple fallacy which may sometimes be concealed, as we shall see (Id.: 26).

Now, as Honderich further pointed out, this is but one of a number of misunderstandings about the nature of desert which have pervaded the conversations and practices of criminal justice until the present day. Others relate to notions of equivalence between the offence and the penalty which imply concepts of equivalence between the two involving proportionality, and which have already been seen to be fragile as the authors of the Justice Model found to their dismay. Yet others concern the suggested and yet uncertain relationship between penalties and the extent of distress caused to those offended against, and thus the form of penalties that might be perceived as 'equalising' the distress. Such an approach involves issues of relative culpability, the antecedent aspects of which would run counter to the retributive approach to punishment.[17]

Punishment as an axiomatic matter of desert is, then, far from the apparently simple equation so frequently encountered in the history of its retributive criminological literature and penal practices. It is the purpose of this book to create a 'distance' between the 'traditional' retributive philosophies and policies which could enable a re-appraisal of the nature of desert in a post-Modern context. In so doing, it may become possible to discern the means by which penal sanctions might be put to a more socially advantageous use, and how this could best be achieved.

In Chapter 3 we shall examine the competing claims of corrective, compensatory and distributive justice, each with its differing interpretations of desert, to a substantive place within criminal (and civil) justice considerations.

---

17 In instances in which, for example, two persons were found to have caused the same extent of distress in committing an offence, the one having acted intentionally and the other accidentally, but in retributive terms both would 'deserve' the same penalty. Such an approach follows the axiom of 'like treatment for like offences', but it becomes questionable where issues of aggravation and mitigation fall to be considered in the sentencing process (see: Gibson, 2009: 21 and 109).

3 Differing Faces of Desert

In this chapter we shall examine a number of different relationships that are commonly held to exist between desert and justice, accepting *a priori* that justice itself is widely perceived as taking three distinctive presentational or institutional forms within contemporary democratic societies. Though this book focuses primarily on criminal (or corrective) justice, it has to be acknowledged that, both actually and conceptually, justice also has, and serves, distributive and compensatory purposes within the daily lives of humankind.

In making this distinction it is not implied that these forms of justice should be considered entirely in isolation, but rather that each contributes somewhat differently to the overall concept of justice developed over the centuries, as we have seen in Chapter 2. Indeed, there are reasons to suggest that corrective, distributive and compensatory forms of justice display aspects of interrelatedness that make them at the least contiguous, if not entirely interdependent.

By way of a shorthand explanation, distributive justice consists in the way in which the institutions of society ensure that benefits and responsibilities or burdens are distributed among its members according to rules and means that are fair and just. Corrective justice relates to the extent that punishments for wrongdoing are also fair and just to the extent of considering relative criteria such as seriousness, criminal intent and culpability. Compensatory justice is concerned with the manner in which citizens are fairly compensated for injuries caused by those who inflict them, and in some or another proportion to the extent of the pain or loss thereby inflicted (cf. Velasquez *et al.*, 1990: 3).

It is also widely accepted within American literature that desert consists in a relationship between three elements: a subject (*i.e.* the focus of the desert); a mode of treatment or state of affairs deserved by the subject; and facts about the subject which are often described as a desert base or bases (see, *e.g.* Velasquez *et al.*, 1990: 2; McLeod, 1999: 61-2; Pojman, 2006: 21; Pojman & McLeod, 1999; Sher, 1987: 7). Summarised algebraically, this relationship can be expressed as: S deserves M by reason of B where S is the subject, M the mode of treatment, and B the desert base(s). We return to this conception of desert and further explanation later.

Distributive Justice

Now, in noting the different forms of justice previously described, we may anticipate that because these forms describe quite different purposes of justice, each may give rise to different forms of desert both in theory and in practice. Thus how societies and their institutions pursue the purposes of distributive justice may vary depending on political, economic, social and historical factors and traditions. These are issues in social policy deliberation and selection which may be far from universal. Moreover, if these policies are adopted on a democratic majority basis and do not violate universally acknowledged concepts and standards of human rights and freedoms, then the policies only become open to criticism in default of delivery in practice.[1]

It may thus be suggested that what individual citizens 'deserve' in democratic distributive justice terms is traceable back to what both Plato and Aristotle somewhat differently described as the social basis of distributive justice as we have previously seen in Chapter 2. In classical terms, therefore, 'it is just for equals to receive equal shares, unjust for equals to receive unequal shares, and unjust for those who are unequal to receive equal shares' as a principle of distributive desert (Plato, 1997b: 1332 BC; Aristotle, 1999: 5.3.1131a10b.16).[2]

Some scholars have observed that the Greek word *axia* as used originally by both Plato and Aristotle to describe the distributions of goods, services and other social benefits can more usefully be translated as meaning 'merit' rather than desert, and might be better understood in that context (*e.g.* Miller, 1999: 125-6). Such an approach would seem to indicate a positive rather than a negative concept of the term 'deserving': a difference that becomes more apparent in considerations of corrective justice to which we now turn.

Corrective (aka Retributive) Justice

Within the context of criminal justice, and in particular in relation to the retributive punishment of offences, the notion of desert has an essentially negative connotation. Both Feldman (1995: 74-76) and Schmidtz (2002: 783-784) draw a clear distinction between desert in distributive and corrective justice on the basis that the former is a forward-looking (and positive) concept, and the latter a backward-looking one – particularly in its retributive interpretation. It might, however, be argued that this amounts to an over-fine distinction, since it fails to accommodate the forward-looking nature of certain other traditionally accepted purposes of criminal punishment such as deterrence, reparation and restoration (or rehabilitation). Indeed, the very term 'corrective' justice suggests a prospective motivation to secure future law-abiding behaviour.

1 Here it must be suggested that, within democracies in which suffrage is universal, citizens have the right to challenge and change the nature of institutions by majority consensus, providing that such consensus is adequately representative in the election of parliamentary officials.

2 The annotated references shown here relate to translations of the works of Plato in *Republic* and Aristotle in *Nicomachean Ethics* respectively.

Punishment practices of a predominantly retributive and backward-looking nature require *deontological* explanations and justifications which assert that either these are a 'good' in themselves or practices required by justice, thus making a claim on our acceptance and compliance. Alternatively, those of a forward-looking nature such as deterrence and restoration require *consequentialist* justifications, probably of a utilitarian nature, as designed to increase overall social benefit by reducing or preventing crime (Bedau & Kelly, 2010: 4). Though hybrid combinations of these interpretations have been advanced by some commentators in recent years in an attempt to avoid this duality by adopting a completely different approach, these have proved largely unsatisfactory (von Hirsch, 1993; Ten, 1987; Hoekema, 1986 among others). There is, however, one notable exception to this observation which lies in the work of John Rawls (1955/1969 Revision).[3]

The definition and justification of punishment as a form of corrective justice must logically accommodate the distinctions noted above, and this in itself is evidently problematic in a number of different respects. Defining punishment conceptually and justifying it in practice are, however, two quite separate but interdependent propositions to which we shall return in greater detail in a later discussion. For the present purposes it must be noted that, insofar as desert is concerned, its confinement to retributive *deontological* justifications of punishment alone is far from a sufficient explanation within this work.

Compensatory Justice

By way of contrast with distributive and corrective justice, compensatory justice concerns the ways in which persons (or organisations) are fairly treated in relation to injuries resulting from wrongdoing by means of compensation.[4] This form of justice is, essentially, of a *consequentialist* utilitarian nature, but brings to the fore the important notion of desert in the form of merit, or as something 'owed' to those harmed by crime as a means of upholding the need for social solidarity and confidence that the law is just to all parties concerned in the commission of offences – whether of a criminal or civil nature (see: Rawls, 1969, in Acton, 1969: 106 in Note 3).

3 In his much quoted paper 'Two Concepts of Rules', originally delivered in 1954 but later revised in 1969 (see, Acton, 1969: 105-114), Rawls advanced an explanation of justified punishment that acknowledged both a retributive (deontological) justification and a utilitarian (consequentialist) alternative consistent with his social contract theory of justice. We shall examine this relationship further in Chapter 4.

4 The term 'injury' used here is not confined to physical harms, but includes forms of loss or damage occasioned by wrongful or negligent acts which may be seen to create an entitlement to compensation. Such compensation may be held to be the responsibility of either the wrongdoer or the state (as the institution of justice) to provide, normally in an extent deemed or assessed to be proportionate to the harm suffered by those injured. Claims to compensation may be resolved in either the civil or criminal courts, in the former as actions for damages, or in the latter as an element of sentencing practice but distinct from fines.

Though compensatory justice need not detain us further at this juncture, it will be evident that it has significant implications for the concepts of reparation and restoration that lie at the core of restorative justice principles, and of mercy (see: Cornwell, 2014a: 49-79; and 2014b *passim*). These important issues are dealt with in greater detail later in this volume.

As a final observation in relation to desert and merit within compensatory justice, it must be acknowledged that both give rise to counter-arguments that cannot lightly be swept aside. David Hume (1983), disputing the validity of desert bases as a reliably comparative means of assessing merit, insisted that judging desert as between individual cases was a fallible concept because the personal native endowments of each and every member of a given society are unknowable (Hume, 1983: 27).[5] Thus the time necessarily spent in ascertaining the extent (or otherwise) of merit in individual cases would have negative consequences.

Some Further Complications in Desert Theory

Given the nature of the differing explanations of desert outlined above, it is at least clear that a consistent theory of desert within the processes of justice must somehow accommodate – to a satisfactory extent – each of these conceptions. Further, that justice, as a social institution of human devising rather than of abstract divination, cannot escape from providing a reasoned justification for including (or excluding) the notion of desert within its practices.

This much stated, scholars have debated over decades past the intriguing question of whether desert should be perceived as having existed *prior to* the emergence of social institutions (pre-institutional desert or p-desert in shorthand), or rather whether it is, in reality, derived from the nature of institutions themselves (institutional desert or i-desert) (cf. *e.g.* Cummiskey, 1987; Celello, undated).[6] P-desert suggests that the concept of desert is a normative construct logically prior to i-desert, without which there would be no means of evaluating the justice of institutions themselves.

Rawls (according to Samuel Scheffler, 2000) rejected pre-justicial desert by insisting that desert can exist only after the principles of justice have been established. Thus, according to Rawls, a person should receive only what justice dictates he should receive. On such a view, desert is not pre-justicial since it is defined, at least in part, in terms of justice. However, justice is normally understood as being pre-institutional since it is a normative concept external to any particular institution, and which can be used to judge or evaluate institutions. The concern here is that defining desert in terms of justice, rather

5 Here, recall the algebraic formulation: S deserves M in virtue of B.

6 See: www.iep.utm.edu/desert/ (Accessed 21 November 2014).

than defining justice in terms of desert results in a 'back to front' understanding of the relationship between the two concepts (Celello, undated: 9).

Either way, this leaves us in a somewhat paradoxical situation in which, ultimately, choices have to be made. Logically, we might accept that justice is pre-institutional in nature, that criminal punishment is an integral element of justice administration, and that desert is a justifying condition of punishment being morally acceptable. Put another way, perhaps, that without desert, criminal punishment as one element of justice would result in both punishment and justice being liable to becoming arbitrary and therefore immoral.

Now, argued from the opposite perspective and defining desert in terms of justice not only negates the notion of its being a pre-institutional concept, but also confines justice to being an institutional construct that cannot therefore be value neutral because it is ultimately derived, or at least prone to being derived from institutional agendas.[7] And since criminal punishment is an operational element of justice, desert defined in terms of justice becomes similarly vulnerable to criticism as an institutional rather than a normative construct and cannot, in such terms, be pre-justicial in nature.[8]

The reader may be wondering why this convoluted discussion is actually important, and if it is important, why it has a bearing on the nature of desert within criminal justice? The answer to these questions lies, I shall suggest, in the way in which punishment, and especially criminal punishment as an outcome of justice, is defined and justified. It is to a discussion of this particular issue that the remaining part of this chapter is devoted.

Punishment: Definitions and Justifications

It is an almost universally accepted tenet of criminal justice that, within liberal constitutional democracies, punishment is an axiomatic outcome of persons being found guilty of violating laws either deliberately or negligently, and with responsibility for having so acted.

7 This is so because institutions are a product of human designing, and are therefore prone to being affected by political, economic or other value-laden considerations. Thus justice removed from its pre-institutional status is liable to being used for instrumental purposes which, if non-moral in operation, would render it incapable of independent evaluation and possibly even unjust.

8 It may assist the reader in understanding the complexity of the foregoing discussion to note that it is based upon a *logical* sequence of argument rather than one of a *time-related* nature. Thus the terms 'pre-institutional' and 'pre-justicial' describe the logical sequence in which justice and desert are philosophically related in concept rather than in time. Therefore, 'pre-institutional' desert implies that it is a prior consideration upon which justice, viewed as an institutional concept, is subsequently formulated. The further implication is that desert is both 'logically prior to, and independent of both tacit and explicit institutional criteria and rules' (Celello, undated: 8). 'Institutional' desert, on the other hand, in the sense argued by Rawls and some others, implies that desert can only logically exist once the principles of justice have been established. Thus, desert in such a sense cannot be 'pre-justicial' since it derives from the prior formulation of the principles of justice (Id.).

In this sense, therefore, punishment is justified by the normative values of these democracies on the one hand, and by the institutionalisation of justice on the other.

It is further generally accepted that laws are a necessary means of regulating the behaviour of citizens in accordance with normative values of acceptable social conduct; that compliance with laws is a precondition of participative citizenship; and that laws will clearly stipulate the nature and extent of sanctions that may legally be imposed on offenders in the event of being adjudged guilty of violation or non-compliance. It is in this manner that both criminal and civil justice are formally institutionalised.

The authority to impose and implement punishment is vested in officials appointed by the state for the specific purposes of ascertaining guilt and its extent or culpability,[9] and for the administration of the sanctions imposed by state-appointed correctional officials on a custodial or non-custodial basis within regulatory powers prescribed and overseen by statute law. Punishment is thus a human institution, deliberately organised and practiced, and explicitly designed to impose some form of deprivation or burden upon those found guilty of offences.[10] It is for these reasons that punishment requires justification.

However, as Bedau and Kelly (2010: 6-7) point out, although punishment can be *defined* without reference to any purposes, it cannot be *justified* without any such reference. Therefore, in seeking a justification of punishment it is necessary to specify or ascertain:

- which goals or purposes are met by establishing and maintaining the practice itself;
- that when punishment is imposed it achieves these goals or purposes;
- that the goals or purposes cannot be met by any other means other than by punishment (in certain ways and not in others);
- that the goals or purposes cannot be achieved with comparable effectiveness and fairness by using other non-punitive forms of intervention; and,
- that achieving these goals and purposes by means of punishment is, in itself, justifiable (Id: 7).

Definitions of punishment have varied over time, some proving more durable than others. One of these more durable explanations is that provided by H.L.A. Hart (1968: 4-5), based upon, and reprinted from his earlier work 'Prolegomenon to the Principles of Punishment' published in 1961 in the *Proceedings of the Aristotelian Society 1959-60*. In what he described as the 'standard case for punishment', Hart insisted that punishment should: 'involve unpleasantness; be for an offence against legal rules; and be of an actual or supposed offender for an offence. It must also be intentionally administered by human beings acting

9 Normally in the form of judges, magistrates or other legal appointees assigned to courts of criminal or civil jurisdiction.

10 In former times these punishments were conceived as inflicting forms of pain or unpleasantness upon offenders as a means of retribution for their offences, and were thus in many instances brutal, excessive and even undeserved.

for an authority constituted by a legal system against which the offence was committed' (Id: 4-5); and see also Cornwell, 2006: 41-43 and Note 1 thereto). Hart's definition was almost identical to that set out by Flew (1954,) and augmented by Benn and Peters (1958), both of which predated him by a few years.

It will be noted here that Hart's definition omits specific mention of an offender having been found guilty of an offence – other than by implication. Neither does it make mention of desert which might at first sight seem surprising. However, as Honderich has indicated, 'desert is a necessary condition of *justified* punishment, but not in itself a sufficient condition. It is necessary, but not enough by itself' (Honderich, 1976: 25) [Italics mine].

Hart's definition of punishment has the virtues of clarity and brevity, while meeting the test of neutrality insofar as it does not introduce or prejudge any issues of policy. And yet on the one hand, punishment is, in effect, still a form of action by the political authority that has jurisdiction in the community in which a harmful wrong may occur. On the other hand, however, justifications of punishment – whether deontological, consequentialist, liberal or a hybrid of these, and expressed in penal policies – may well be politically value laden to a considerable extent.[11]

Predominantly retributive justifications of punishment are especially prone to failure since it has hitherto proved impossible to devise a non-arbitrary means of determining with any precision how much punishment (in sentencing terms) is proportionate or deserved in relation to the gravity of offences falling within differing categories of crime. Put another way, there is no non-arbitrary way of identifying the just points of maximum and minimum severity defining the penalty schedule, or the intervals between adjacent offences and punishments (Pincoffs, 1977: 75-88).

The Purposes of Punishment

The criticism of retributive justifications cited above suggests very strongly the need to examine closely the purposes that are proposed for establishing and maintaining the practice of punishment, and how these are justified both theoretically and in practice. The criminological literature is replete with explanations of the purposes of, and supposed justifications of, retribution, deterrence (both general and specific), rehabilitation and, in earlier decades, reform which have universally been accepted as the principal purposes of criminal punishment. I have surveyed these purposes in some considerable detail in earlier work (Cornwell, 2006: 41-79) with particular reference to the leading authorities whose works have contributed notably to these debates, and therefore a full-scale repetition of

11 In particular, where forms of criminal punishment are specifically designed in sentencing terms to be predominantly retributive or incapacitative. This includes the practice of detaining offenders, on predictions of future dangerousness, on an indeterminate or extended sentence basis in the interests of public protection.

this account is superfluous in this book. In what follows here, I shall, however, provide a summary of the main problematic aspects of these explanations insofar as these have a direct bearing upon considerations of desert, and, in addition, provide a summary explanation of the *naissance* of restorative justice from its comparatively contemporary beginnings in the late 1970s and into the present millennium.

Retributive Justice Theory

The backward-looking nature of the retributive concept of criminal punishment, focused as it is on past offences and the necessity that these be punished, has proved remarkably durable and persuasive even in post-Modern criminology. It is, as Bedau and Kelly (2010: 8) have rightly indicated, 'based upon two *a priori* norms (the first that the guilty deserve to be punished, and the second that no moral consideration outweighs the offender's criminal desert), and an epistemological claim (that we can determine with reasonable certainty what and how much punishment the guilty deserve)' (Primoratz, 1989; Moore, 1987).

As we have seen previously, however, these apparently self-evident deontological assertions are distinctly questionable since it is arguable whether the guilty *always* do deserve punishment, whether they ought *always* to get what they 'deserve', and even when they are punished, whether the punisher *always* knows what they deserve – other than in a procedural sense (Bedau, 1978). We return to this contentious issue later in this work, but the reader will note, and possibly even reject, the underpinning assumption of retributive theory that the laws whose violation make offenders *eligible* for punishment invariably protect genuine individual rights.

Retributive justice may have retained an intuitive appeal to the uncritical mind because of its apparently indisputable 'rightness', but its inherent fundamental assumptions are, at least in certain instances, evidently fragile. The further problem that arises from this situation is the distinct danger that retributive punishment is prone to being used instrumentally insofar as it 'legitimises' the use of offenders as a *means* towards social control, rather than *ends* in themselves.[12]

Deterrence: The Legal Threat in Crime Control

Deterrence theories and their associated social and penal policy prescriptions may, like those of a retributive nature considered above, have a similarly intuitive appeal. Whether

12 Such is to suggest that the supposed purpose of criminal justice is to exercise a corrective influence towards future law-abiding and pro-social conduct, rather than vicariously as a means of crime control through the threat of retaliation via punishment.

of a 'specific' or of a general nature,[13] it will be evident to most thinking observers of criminal justice that the extent to which deterrent policies are successful in practice is altogether unknowable. Whether or not human beings, either individually or collectively, desist from offending or re-offending may or may not be influenced by deterrent policies at all or to any significant extent. Indeed, if they do desist, this may be for any number of reasons – such as the relative likelihood of detection – which have no specific or measurable relationship with sentencing for the purposes of deterrence.

Curiously, deterrence as a forward-looking notion has to be justified on a consequentialist basis, and yet it is frequently linked with deontologically justified and backward-looking retribution theory as a purpose of criminal punishment. Such a 'two-eyed' stance may suggest a 'win either way' approach to justice that has a certain policy-formulation appeal, but since both supposed purposes are conceptually and operationally flawed it becomes difficult to perceive them as morally or ethically sustainable within democratic societies. One thing can, however, be incontrovertibly stated: deterrence as a supposed purpose of criminal justice and punishment has absolutely no congruence with, or relationship to, desert.

The Rehabilitative Ethic: A Relic of Antiquity?

As we have seen in Chapter 1, the demise of rehabilitative approaches within the purposes of criminal punishment occurred during the 1970s with its prospective replacement by the 'Justice Model'of corrections – at least in the USA and in Britain. Whether or not this almost entire abandonment was premature remains a matter of some debate, particularly since the rehabilitative ethic enjoyed (albeit briefly) a measure of resurgence with the demise of the 'Justice Model' during the late 1980s, and yet again in Britain in the criminological and political discourses in the present decade.[14]

13 Specific deterrence applies to the individual offender on the basis that the nature and extent of the punishment meted out to him/her will deter the person from future offending. General deterrence, on the other hand, is based on the supposed 'preventive' effect on other 'would be' offenders that witnessing the punishment of actual offenders might have, and that this would encourage desistence.

14 In early 2012, the then Lord Chancellor and Justice Secretary, Kenneth Clarke, launched a consultative Green Paper (Ministry of Justice, 2012a). This document proposed a radical reform of the use of short term prison custody combined with a significant overhaul of community sentences and the role of the National Probation Services in England and Wales. The consultation period was relatively brief in duration (27 March – 22 June 2012), but the proposals aroused considerable disquiet within the agencies of the criminal justice system, and the Judiciary and the National Probation Service in particular, due to the extensive nature of the reforms proposed. The outcome became evident in the somewhat peremptory replacement of Kenneth Clarke as Justice Secretary, and the Green Paper proposals were effectively abandoned. It would appear that Clarke's putative reforms were regarded as electorally unfavourable by a Conservative-dominated coalition government, failed to gain the support of his Cabinet colleagues, and thus led to his speedy replacement as Justice Secretary.

In terms of desert considerations, neo-rehabilitative purposes of criminal punishment, with the consequentialist (or utilitarian) motivations that these imply, run entirely counter to the prevailing and retributively punitive culture of crime control in a number of Western-style democracies. Such a situation makes rehabilitative initiatives electorally unattractive to governments anxious to be perceived as 'tough on crime', and therefore prone to pursue criminal justice policies with greater resonance for the 'law and order' lobbies and the sensationalist sentiments of the mass media.

However politically unattractive and electorally sensitive rehabilitative motivations may seem, these do introduce an entirely different consequentialist concept of desert with criminal justice. Rather than accepting the primary retributive assumption concerning the axiomatic nature of punishment as deserved, the rehabilitative approach suggests that in many instances those who commit offences are in need of, and therefore deserve, substantial assistance and encouragement to become law abiding, and this assistance to a greater extent than automatic recourse to punitive measures. We shall examine the appropriateness of such interpretations of justice later in this work.

Restorative Justice: A Bridge Too Far?

Mention was made earlier in this Chapter of the emergence of the concept of restorative justice from the late 1970s and onwards, and in particular during the 1990s and into this millennium, as a worldwide conception of 'doing justice better' (Eglash, 1977; Zehr, 1990 and 2002; Wright, 1992; Zehr & Mika, 1998 among others). It is a conception of justice that is not anti-retributivist (as has been claimed by some observers), but it has a distinctive utilitarian motivation that is proposed in a contemporary *consequentialist* manner distinctly different from that of earlier utilitarian thinkers from Bentham to Rawls.

Restorative justice focuses on the responsibility of offenders to repair the damage caused by their offences by taking responsibility for their wrongful actions, showing genuine remorse, making apology for them to their victims, and making reparation both to the victims themselves, and to the communities harmed by their unlawful acts. Proponents of restorative justice maintain that although consequences in the form of sanctions have to follow from illegal acts, those offenders who demonstrate willingness to make amends for their conduct deserve the opportunity to make good (insofar as possible) the harm caused through substantive reparation as a means of being restored to normal citizenship within their communities (Cornwell, 2007 *passim*; 2009: xxv; 2014a: 99-100).

Such a concept suggests, and indeed insists, that desert be seen to operate in a dualistic manner: on the one hand that offenders deserve the opportunity (when appropriate) to make good the harm caused by crime; and on the other hand that victims of crime deserve the reparation made by offenders as a means of redressing the harm or distress caused to them, and of restoring the social disequilibrium caused by crime. In the next chapter we shall examine in more detail how this concept as a purpose of criminal justice might make it possible to reframe desert and be given a less equivocal interpretation than those described thus far in this discussion.

This chapter has, however, demonstrated that interpretation and acceptance of desert within criminal justice as a self-evident and axiomatic retributive response to offences can be misleading and in certain circumstances largely unhelpful. It has further shown that the nature of desert can be differently conceived within other interpretations of justice. The remaining part of this work will adopt a more forward-looking approach to describing how this historically negative legacy might be remedied in the future.

4 Revising the Algebra

Challenging the 'Traditional' Desert Calculus

Early in the preceding chapter, brief reference was made to Celello's explanation of desert within criminal punishment in an algebraic formula 'S deserves M in virtue (or by reason) of B' (Celello, undated: 2), a concept widely endorsed by writers such as Sher, 1987: 7; McLeod, 1999: 61-62; Pojman, 2006: 21 and others. While at first sight such a formulation might appear to be unexceptionable, it may be seen to have been co-opted within retributive approaches to criminal justice as a justifying aspect of penal policies and practices designed primarily to deliver punishment and crime control through incapacitation via extended and indeterminate sentencing.

In this chapter an attempt will be made to challenge the morality of adopting such a basis for justifying penal policies and practices, and to suggest that other and less unacceptable interpretations of the formula would lead logically to a more inclusive and effective approach to crime reduction as a central purpose of criminal justice. It will also be suggested that the concept of restorative justice described briefly in the concluding section of Chapter 3 might provide the means of achieving such a transition.

As we have seen in earlier chapters, the dominance of retributive penal policies occurred to a considerable extent by default: disenchantment with rehabilitative approaches, the demise of the Justice Model of corrections, and increasing scepticism in relation to deterrence created a philosophical vacuum in which retribution alone seemed the only credible option for policy determination. Thus, to punish and to do so more severely became an attractive resort despite the inherent difficulties of doing so proportionately. Meanwhile, however, deterrence retained some intuitive appeal since it had a forward-looking motivation that meshed to some extent with utilitarian explanations, however un-measurable its effects in practice (Box, 1981; Bean, 1981: 29-31 and *passim*).

All of this left desert considerations within criminal justice in a somewhat parlous state since it became inextricably associated with retribution in a negative context (cf. Kristjánsson (2003: 41).[1] Offenders thus became viewed as undeserving of anything other than punishment, largely regardless of any circumstances of social disadvantage or normlessness in which many of them evidently existed, and which were widely held to be causative of crime (cf. *e.g.* Becker, 1963; Matza, 1969, among many others).

1 Positive desert, on the other hand, was perceived by Kristjánsson and others as deserving of some entitlement to praise, reward, remuneration and the like derived from success, productivity, or some other measure of effort or performance.

As has become evident also, adoption of predominantly retributive sentencing policies has resulted in a widespread escalation of penal populations held in custody, and for increasing periods of time. In addition, where such policies appear to reduce rates of recorded and convicted recidivist crime,[2] there has been some equivocation about the extent to which these are assessed and calculated on a consistent basis.

The Axiomatic Retributive Algebra

The preceding observations notwithstanding, it is necessary to take seriously the contemporary retributive algebra of criminal punishment which has achieved a dominance largely undisputed since the demise of the Justice Model during the 1980s and onwards. This algebraic proposition may be summarised as:

> **O deserves P by reason of CG**
> Where O is an offender, P is punishment and CG the gravity of his crime

A claim of this nature with its appeal to human sentiment may, at face value, be seen as unexceptionable on the basis that a law has been broken, and that the perpetrator of that act deserves punishment to some or another extent consistent or commensurate with the gravity of the 'wrongness' committed.

Now, since this debate concerns an important issue within criminal justice we should, at the least, test it against accepted standards of examination in relation to those of moral and ethical probity that we have inherited in the classical discourses that were, to a considerable extent, more apolitical than those of our contemporary understanding.[3] This implies that there may be differences between the natures of a classical 'absolutist' approach to defining principles of moral behaviour on the one hand, and what has, within contemporary conversations about morality, become a 'customary' interpretation of the same basic principles on the other.[4]

2 As measured in recidivism statistics that retrospectively measure the rates of reconviction of offenders subsequent to the expiry of sentences (cf. *e.g.* Prison Reform Trust, 2013: 2-3 and *passim*; Ministry of Justice, 2013a). There is, for example, a considerable difference between cases in which an offender is reconvicted for the same crime as that previously committed, and those in which other and possibly lesser crimes are committed and for which the offender is subsequently convicted.

3 The term 'morality' is derived from the 14th century Latin term *moralis* relating to a system of moral and ethical principles of customary behaviour involving distinctions between right and wrong, good and bad. Ethics is the philosophical study of the moral *value* of human conduct, and the rules or principles that ought to govern it. Though dictionary definitions of such matters differ marginally, these are taken from Collins English Dictionary, 1979, on pp. 502 and 1165 respectively.

4 The reasons for this differentiation are important within the debate that follows. For as we have seen in Chapter 2, concepts of justice in general and punishment in particular have changed considerably over time. Whereas the Code of Hammurabi prescribed capital punishment for a number of offences of both a criminal

In earlier work (Cornwell, 2014b: 27-29) I have sketched working definitions of justice and equity, and of the relationship between these two in terms of impartiality, fairness and reasonableness. Though both display evident similarities, equity includes one particular and important characteristic: that of introducing 'an element of interpretive discretion in pursuit of fairness, allowing the spirit of the law to override its literal meaning in circumstances unusual or unforeseen' (Id: 28-29).[5]

Within ethics, justice is the moral principle that determines the fairness of actions, and within law it consists in its administration in terms of legal validity, and according to prescribed and accepted principles. Such leads inevitably to consideration of desert within the narrower context of penology, since it involves pivotal and yet conflicting issues of principle that affect both the workings and the outcomes of the processes of justice in practice.

Returning now to our previous algebraic formulation of contemporary retributive justice (O deserves P by reason of CG) in the light of the foregoing discussion, we may now assess its implications, at least in terms of justice, equity and morality, both conceptually and operationally. In so doing, we may also ascertain the nature of desert subsumed within such a formulation.

Is the Retributive Formulation Just?

It will be recalled that the proposition in question is that offenders (O) deserve punishment (P) by reason of the gravity of their crimes (CG), where O is the subject, P the mode of treatment, and CG the desert base. Now, had a prior finding of guilt been specified rather than assumed, this could have been added as a second desert base in the circumstances, without prejudice to the nature of the proposition.

What has to be established in relation to its 'justness' is whether or not the proposition as an assertion is universally true in the first place, and then subsequently whether it is impartial, fair and reasonable in distributive terms.[6] To be universally true it would need to be shown that it is invariably the case that *all* offenders deserve punishment, and also that the relative gravity of their offences can be discerned with sufficient precision (as within and between different forms of offending) to be both fair and reasonable.

---

and civil nature, and this 'talionic' approach was to a greater or lesser extent persistent until the Enlightenment Era of the 18th century. 'Customary' modes of moral and ethical philosophical thinking thereafter led to a considerable modification of such 'extremist' views.

5 Thus equity includes the consideration of circumstances that reasonably necessitate or obligate leniency (Lauchs, 2005: 2), and, by implication, of aggravation also.

6 The word 'distributive' as intended here refers to the processes by which justice is administered in practice in the form of sanctions or punishments for wrongdoing.

Within the Anglo-Saxon tradition of law at least, it is generally accepted that offenders suffering from certain forms and extents of mental illness or impairment such as to limit their responsibility may be excluded from the general provisions of criminal law (Gibson, 2009: 105-107). Such persons are, therefore, discounted from consideration in this discussion.

In the more general sense, however, it has been widely maintained that offenders with significant social deficits[7] deserve assistance to enable them to live law-abiding lives in the future. The following table provides an indication of the deficits of adult prisoners in England and Wales by comparison with the general population.

Table 4: 1 Social Characteristics of Adult Prisoners (England and Wales) 2012 – Compared with the General Population

Characteristic	Prison Population %	General Population %
Taken into care as a child	24% (31% F; 24% M)	2%
Expelled or permanently excluded from school	42% (32% F; 43%M)	>1% (2005 England)
No qualifications	47%	15% of working age population
Unemployed in the four weeks before custody	68% (81% F: 67%M)	7.7% of economically active unemployed
Never had a job	13%	3.9%
Homeless before entering custody	15%	4% have been homeless or in temporary accommodation
Have symptoms indicative of psychosis	16% (25% F; 15%M)	4%
Identified as suffering both anxiety and depression	25% (49% F; 15%M)	15%
Have attempted suicide at some time	30% (46% F; 21%M)	6%
Have ever used Class A drugs	64%	13%

Source: Extracted from Prison Reform Trust (2014: 31)
The Prison Reform Trust (2014) lists all the sources of data for both the prison population and the general population used in its compilation in its own footnotes on p. 31.

From the table shown above, it will be clearly evident that adult prisoners in England and Wales in particular present a profile of social disadvantage considerably more extensive than that of the general population. In terms of home background also, many more have experienced abuse as children (29:20%), have observed violence in the home (41:14%),

7 Such as long term unemployment, homelessness, symptoms of mental impairment, drug or substance dependency, and lack of qualifications to gain employment compared with the general population (Prison Reform Trust, 2014: 31).

and regularly truanted from school (59:5.2%). Furthermore, 54% of adult prisoners have children who are under the age of 18, compared with approximately 27% of the adult population aged 18 or over (Office for National Statistics, 2012, 2013: tables).

In assessing the fairness of the contemporary retributive response to crime, two central issues have to be considered: first, whether it is morally defensible; and second, whether it results in equitable justice. For as we have previously seen, the nature of justice administration as prescribed in statute law[8] has changed in a cyclic manner since the immediate post-World War II era. The penal policies and their underpinning ideologies deemed appropriate during the dominance of the rehabilitative ethic became supplanted by those of the 'just deserts' model of proportionality during the 1970s and 1980s, only to return to the predominantly retributive and deterrence-based *mantra* of the 1990s and onwards. What did not change significantly over these decades of increasing general material affluence was the evident and widespread persistence of social disadvantage and lesser eligibility among the poorest and most deprived elements of the modern societies in which crime was, and continues to be, an endemic phenomenon.

This is not to suggest that social disadvantage and relative poverty are excuses for law breaking, since all citizens within democratic societies are deemed to be equally liable to be law abiding (the doctrine of equality under the law), but it does imply that those thus placed may find temptation to commit crime more difficult to resist as a means of redressing their feelings of social inequality and marginalisation. Here the reader may recall the words of the French novelist Anatole France (1844-1924) who remarked: 'The law, in its majestic equality, forbids the rich as well as the poor to sleep under bridges, to beg in the streets, and to steal their bread'.[9] To which it might be added that while the rich might not wish or need to behave thus, the poor might find avoiding doing so rather more difficult.

The moral dilemma into which we are propelled here is, at the least, profound. For if we are to insist, as the retributive algebra would compel, that all wrongdoing deserves punishment irrespective of who commits it, then we should surely also accept that the punishment of the already disadvantaged is of a different punitive quality from that imposed upon those not so burdened. Even further, if we persist in punishing in such a manner, then that imposed upon the former is unequal to that imposed on the latter, and is therefore both unjust and immoral.

In such a situation, however, equitable treatment would suggest that the disadvantaged are actually deserving of something other than mere punishment in order to assist them to live law-abiding lives and resist the temptation to re-offend. This logically implies

8 The technical legality of which is largely unquestionable since it expresses the sovereign will of the democratic parliamentary process in most Western-style national circumstances.

9 France (1894, in Chapter 7).

making available to such offenders the means of addressing their social deficits, and the encouragement and assistance to do so. But because this means alternative forms of capital investment other than building more and more prisons,[10] the concept does not sit easily alongside the prevailing retributive rhetoric of post-modern penology focused upon crime control. We shall return to this concept later in this work.

It is, of course, an evident fact that many offenders do not have personal histories of social disadvantage of the nature or extent revealed in Table 4: 1, that they offend as a matter of personal choice, from a variety of different motivations, and that they are, or could be held to be, aware of the potential consequences of their actions – whether or not they consider these consequences when committing criminal acts. Some offend more seriously than others, even though it has historically proved difficult to determine, other than approximately, the extent to which the seriousness or gravity of crimes differs within and between different categories of offending.[11]

The Outcomes

Acceptance of the retributive algebra would inevitably lead to a questioning of the nature and extent of 'punishment' that we are compelled to impose upon convicted offenders in response to the relative seriousness of the crimes that they commit. It would also open up a further debate about what punishment consists in, or rather, perhaps, what mode(s) of treatment might be considered as an appropriate response to an offence, given the circumstances of the offender and, therefore, what he/she most deserves in order to reduce the likelihood of further offending. The retributive agenda would insist that the response be essentially punitive,[12] while the consequentialist (or utilitarian) response would focus primarily upon modes of treatment or training more likely to induce future behavioural change.

10 Such is to suggest investment in considerably enhanced community correctional services in terms of both infrastructure and professional training, designed to deliver remedial and training support combined with actual work experience programmes within local communities as an alternative to short-term imprisonment.

11 For while we might intuitively consider, for example, murder to be more serious than certain manslaughter offences, and armed robbery more serious than aggravated burglary, it remains difficult to place offences such as rape, arson, blackmail, fraud, kidnapping, causing actual bodily harm or buggery in any precise hierarchy of offences in order of relative seriousness and, therefore, desert of punishment.

12 Such as to involve 'pain' or unpleasantness as a means of encouraging future desistance through specific (or individual) deterrence. Hence, therefore, the retributive reliance upon wide use of incapacitation through sentences of imprisonment.

A Different View of the Equation

All of the foregoing discussion stated, however, retributive pre-occupation with the offender neglects altogether a dimension of desert in relation to criminal and other offences which is of significant importance. All offences cause harm to a greater or lesser extent, and this harm involves some person(s) or entities in suffering the effects of the wrongful act on an involuntary basis. Somehow, therefore, our revised algebra should take due account of this situation, since it could be said to create a different form of desert as merited by those offended against.

Following the logic of the original proposition, we might propose a second equation in the following terms:

> **V deserves R by reason of CG**
> Where V is the victim, R denotes reparation, and GC the gravity of the crime

Expanded somewhat, our new proposition suggests that victims of crime deserve some form of reparation or compensation relative to the gravity of the crime committed against them and the extent of the harm suffered as a result.

Viewed in relation to the original proposition it will be noted that (following *e.g.* Kristjánsson, 2003: 41) we have now established two quite different forms or modes of treatment: in the former case the *negative* and backward-looking mode of retributive justice, and in the present case a *positive* and prospective mode within a form of distributive justice (see here also Celello, undated: 3).[13] In this particular instance, however, the desert base is identical in either proposition (*i.e.* the gravity of crime), and the two are therefore construed as being strictly commensurable for the purposes of this work.

Traditionally, at least within the Anglo-Saxon conception of justice administration, it has been the province of the criminal courts predominantly to enquire into allegations or accusations of criminal offending according to the evidence made available, to establish whether those so accused are guilty or innocent, and to punish the guilty in accordance with the sentencing provisions of statute law. It has also been left, in the main, to the courts

13 Here it should be noted that there has been some semantic debate within the philosophical literature concerning a perceived difference between the terms 'desert' and 'merit', and also the concepts of retrospective and prospective desert. Some scholars (*e.g.* Miller, 1976: 93; Rachels, 1997: 176, and Feinberg, 1970: 70) have argued that desert is strictly retrospective in nature, while others (*e.g.* Feldman, 1995, and Schmidtz, 2002) have contended that desert can be prospective, and indeed is so in relation to compensation where the desert base is legitimately grounded in the extent of harm occasioned. McLeod (1999: 67) has maintained that in ordinary usage the terms desert and merit are used interchangeably, and therefore the supposed distinction between the two is largely unhelpful and unnecessary.

of civil law to determine claims for compensation arising out of criminal and other injuries under the laws of torts and damages.[14]

The Dilemma of Competing Ethical Values

Given the two algebraic propositions or constructions of desert described in the foregoing discussion, it becomes apparent that many justice systems, and at least a number of those within the Anglo-Saxon tradition, are presently faced with a fundamental ethical dilemma arising out of the concept of desert.[15] This situation arises because on the one hand 'traditional' retrospective criminal justice policies aimed at crime control, and based upon primarily retributive punishment of offenders and incapacitation, not only fail significantly to reduce recidivist crime, but also lead to escalating prison populations . On the other hand, prospective policies aimed at crime reduction and based upon reparative justice and victim-consciousness have proven to be more effective and less costly, but have limited political appeal to governments and political leaders anxious to be seen to be 'tough on crime'.

From an ethical perspective it is possible to justify the retributive algebra on an intuitive deontological basis that crime deserves punishment if, and only if, it can be shown that the guilty always do deserve punishment, that the system that delivers punishment is just,[16] and that other than in an entirely procedural sense the process actually achieves its stated purposes. These evident difficulties apart, there remains that of conceiving a non-arbitrary means of determining what form of punishment and to what actual extent guilty offenders deserve to be punished – particularly as between different forms of offending. The retributive algebra has proved justifiably vulnerable to criticism in a number of these respects.

The alternative victim-focused proposition discussed earlier is clearly of a consequentialist (or utilitarian) nature that may, at first sight, appear to be only distantly, if at all, related to the retributive one. However, this is not necessarily the case for reasons that deserve explanation. First, it will be noted that the gravity of the crime (and therefore the harm caused by it) is common to both algebraic formulations. Second, there is a relationship between offenders and victims of crime, the former as those causing harm, and the latter

14 There are, however, certain provisions within the criminal law of the United Kingdom in which the courts have powers to make ancillary orders for compensation which must precede any other sentence or order such as a fine or community sentence (see: Gibson, 2009: 42). The Criminal Injuries Compensation Authority (CICA) operates a scale of payments that it can make to victims of violence where adequate court-based compensation is not obtained (Id.).

15 Here it will be recalled that ethical considerations involve the philosophical study of the moral values of human conduct, and of the rules or principles that ought to govern it.

16 'Just' in the sense of meeting stringent tests of behavioural morality in principle and in operation.

as those directly harmed as a result. This relationship, however tenuous or indistinct, contains a potential for positive and remedial activity on either side. Third, the nature of the desert in either case need not be as mutually exclusive as might, superficially, be imagined.

By way of explaining these seemingly incongruous relationships, it may be helpful to examine a number of aspects of criminal (and other) offending as it actually occurs in our experiences of everyday life. Not all offenders are wicked, calculating, ruthless and remorseless predators motivated by greed or malicious intent to cause harm or misery to others. Many are tempted into committing offences as a potential means of somehow reducing their perceptions of social disadvantage or inequality, or because they lack the social and life skills and competencies necessary to compete in contemporary societies in a law-abiding manner. Some are disadvantaged from birth in one or more of the aspects highlighted in Table 4: 1 previously discussed, while others are lured by the prospect of short-term gratification of their perceived 'needs' or by peer group pressure, and entirely discount the likelihood of being detected. Many fewer are the calculating, predatory and brutal villains depicted in media crime scene presentations.

A considerable number of relatively lower-level offenders,[17] once confronted with the harm and distress caused by their offences, are genuinely remorseful and willing to make apology and amends to victims of these offences given an opportunity to do so. They are also amenable, if enabled to do so, to redress their deficits through skills training and counselling to enable them to resist the temptation to re-offend.

Victims of offences, on the other hand, may express deeply felt anger, resentment, or a sense of violation, trauma or other emotional distress in relation to those who have offended against them. In many such instances the expression of apology, genuine remorse and offer of reparation by offenders can alleviate their adverse situations to a considerable extent. The retributive agenda of punishment as axiomatically deserved is less concerned about the plight of victims than the necessity for a punitive response to offences, and as a result victims become marginalised in considerations of desert.

The question of concern within this work is that of which of the two propositions has the greater moral merit in relation to the delivery of true justice and the reduction of crime. Traditional retributive punishment neither requires nor expects that offenders express remorse in respect of their offences, or make any apology or reparation to those whom they have harmed. That they must be punished to some or another extent according to the assessed gravity of their offences requites the law, however imprecise the means of assessment may be, or the relative relationship between the seriousness of different offences and, therefore, the extent or duration of the punishment imposed.

---

17 Such, for example, as thieves, burglars, shoplifters, and those with addictions to drugs, alcohol or other substances, or who are homeless vagrants reliant upon social support or charity.

Reparative justice, by way of contrast, assumes a relationship of some positive nature between offenders and victims of crime, and it is this relationship that has the potential to enable offenders to achieve restoration to law-abiding citizenship while at the same time being inclusive of victims and vindicating or ameliorating their feelings of harm and trauma. It is also more accommodating of discretionary interpretation within the spirit of the law, which is the essence of equitable sanctioning.

The concept of competing ethical values implies that these important considerations should be rigorously assessed as a means of evaluating the morality of criminal punishment. It has also exposed the differences between deontological and consequentialist approaches within penology, an understanding of which has indicated the extent to which desert is capable of variable interpretation within the scholarly discourses of criminal justice administration. In the chapter that follows, we shall explore how these issues may enable us to discern why and how a paradigm shift in contemporary criminal justice has become essential if these differences are to be overcome in the interests of 'doing justice better'.

5 Justice at the Crossroads

The Contemporary Scenario

In the concluding part of the previous chapter the reader was confronted with a choice between two paradigms of criminal justice – the retributive and the reparative – based upon different conceptual interpretations of the nature of desert, and invited to consider which of the two had the greater moral merit. The traditional and still dominant retributive explanation of desert as expressed in the contemporary penal politics and policies in Britain and certain other Western-style democracies has proved remarkably resistant to change in spite of its evident philosophical flaws; this combines with failure to deliver either crime control or significant reductions in recidivism – particularly among consistently increasing numbers of offenders imprisoned for their crimes.

The reparative explanation of desert as articulated in particular in the restorative justice movement's approach to criminal justice has attracted increasing support from academia and professional practitioners during the past two decades. It is, to an extent, a utilitarian alternative strategy for crime reduction involving less reliance upon imprisonment and wider use of community-based sanctions. However, it differs most significantly from the retributive agenda in its victim inclusiveness and community participation in seeking crime reduction and lower rates of recidivism. The model might also be described as a 'responsibility' paradigm since it requires offenders to accept responsibility for the harm caused to those whom they victimise, and to make amends to them through apology and reparation as a means to their eventual restoration to full and law-abiding citizenship.

Many contemporary criminal justice systems exist in some measure of crisis or 'overload' due to the pressure of 'numbers' in penal custody, the fiscal costs of 'containing' these populations, and the high rates of re-offending relatively soon after offenders have been released from prisons. In times of relative economic hardship, these costs can become an unacceptably severe burden on national resources, diverting financial capacity away from other and more desirable social expenditure sources such as health, education and much-needed environmental and infrastructural initiatives. It remains a most curious socio-economic paradox that governments continue to meet these high and increasingly demanding penal costs when to do so is to a very considerable extent avoidable.

In this chapter we shall examine some of the main reasons why so many democratic governments in this new millennium continue to absorb such excessive and unnecessary costs of criminal justice administration.[1] Such an analysis becomes essential to this work because it will, to a considerable extent, reveal why persistence with the retributive desert model of criminal punishment at the core of penal policies makes such expenditure both inevitable and unavoidable. Moreover, only by understanding this cause and effect relationship will it be possible to propose why alternative strategies are fast becoming not only desirable but also essential to the future welfare and fiscal stability of many post-Modern democracies.

Prisons and Prisoners in England and Wales – An Analysis

At the time of writing, there are 118 prisons in England and Wales,[2] and of these prisons eighty were technically overcrowded to some extent in late September 2014.[3] On 10 October 2014 the prison population stood at 84,485, an increase of 73.76% compared with the 1994 level of 48,621. Between 2002 and 2014 this average daily population increased by 14,291 (20.0%) despite the fact that the numbers held on remand (un-convicted or un-sentenced) fell by 7%, while those sentenced to immediate custody rose by 25% (Prison Reform Trust, 2014: 4 and 18; Ministry of Justice, 2014a: Table A1.2). As a result of these increases, England and Wales alone within the UK now have an imprisonment rate of 149 *per* hundred thousand of the population compared with France (102) and Germany (81) *per* hundred thousand (ICPS, 2014).[4]

In terms of sentencing outcomes, average sentence lengths have been increasing since 2004 and now stand at 15.5 months, three months longer than in 2004. The proportion of the sentenced population serving life or other indeterminate sentences has doubled from 9% in 1993 to 18% in 2014 (Ministry of Justice, 2013a; 2014a: Tables A1.1 and A1.12.). In

---

1 The penal system of England and Wales will be used a baseline for this evaluation, using statistical data and explanatory information made available by the Prison Reform Trust (2014) in the format of its Bromley Briefings with full supporting references to government and parliamentary sources as necessary from its Autumn 2014 Edition (Full Version) available at: www.prisonreformtrust.org.uk by selecting Bromley Briefing 2014 Autumn.

2 In January 2015, the total number of prisons changes frequently as a result of older prisons being closed and new generation prisons being commissioned, built and opened. Current emphasis is being placed on the closure of smaller and cost-intensive prisons, and their replacement by much larger establishments as a means of producing economies of scale and reducing staffing costs while meeting increasing demand for prison places.

3 Criteria for overcrowding are measured in two main respects. The certified normal accommodation (CNA) level of a prison is that level of prisoner occupancy for which it was originally designed and commissioned. More recently in times of overcrowding above CNA, what has been termed the operational capacity of each prison is defined as 'the total number of prisoners (using *e.g.* cell sharing in cells designed for single occupancy) that a prison can hold without serious risk to security, good order, and the proper operation of the planned regime' (Prison Service Order 1900 – Certified Prisoner Accommodation).

4 The population of France is almost the same size as that of the United Kingdom, while that of Germany is 20 million larger.

addition, the average time served by those serving mandatory life sentences[5] increased from 13 to 17 years between 2001 and 2013 (Ministry of Justice, 2014b: Table A3.4; Id. 2010). It is also of interest to note here that, in September 2012, England and Wales had the highest number (7,674) of prisoners serving life sentences in Europe – more than France, Germany and Italy combined (4,084) (Council of Europe, 2013: Table 7). At the end of June 2014, of those serving life sentences 1,974 had a tariff length of less than 10 years, 4,006 a tariff length of between 10 and 20 years, and 1,204 a tariff length of more than 20 years. In addition, a further 48 prisoners were serving 'whole life' tariff periods (Prison Reform Trust, 2014: 23 and see Note 6 below).

The indeterminate sentence for public protection (ISPP), which was established in the Criminal Justice Act 2003 and became available from 4 April 2004, has been abandoned as part of the Legal Aid, Sentencing and Punishment of Offenders Act 2012. However, at the end of June 2014 there were still 5,119 prisoners serving an ISPP sentence of whom 3,620 were serving beyond their tariff dates (Prison Reform Trust, 2014: 24; Ministry of Justice, 2014c: Table 1.9).[6] The sentence was available for certain serious violent or sexual offenders assessed as presenting a risk of future dangerousness to the public, and on conviction of offences carrying a maximum penalty of ten years imprisonment or more (see: Gibson, 2009: 87).

In place of the ISPP, a new sentence – the extended determinate sentence (EDS) –has been created within the same Act, under the provisions of which those convicted of serious violent or sexual crimes remain in prison for at least two-thirds of their sentence, with an extended period on licence on release of up to five years for violent offences and eight years for sexual offences.

At the other end of the sentencing spectrum and in the year ending March 2014, 57% of all custodial sentences were for six months or less, and 34,606 offenders were given sentences of up to and including three months in duration (Ministry of Justice, 2014d: Table Q5.5).

Remand Prisoners – A Particular Category

In the twelve months to March 2014, 49,304 people were remanded into prison custody to await trial. In the same period, 33,585 persons were remanded in prisons having been

5 Mandatory life sentences apply to the crime of murder and certain other, though rare, offences of ancient origin such as treason and arson in HM Dockyards which remain in the statute law.

6 Tariff periods are set by the courts at the time of sentencing, and relate to that portion of the sentence deemed necessary to satisfy punishment and retribution. Thereafter, release of prisoners thus sentenced is at the discretion of the Parole Board, but they may remain on licence (and liable to recall to prison custody) indefinitely. However, unlike life sentences, such offenders can apply to have their licences reviewed ten years after release.

convicted and awaiting sentence (Ministry of Justice, 2014e: Table 2.2a). At the end of June 2014 the average daily remand population in prisons was 12,917, an increase of 11% on the previous year due to the larger number of prisoners awaiting trial (875) and sentence (371) (Ministry of Justice, 2014e: Table 1.1). Of these prisoners, 10,832 (11%) were subsequently acquitted, and a further 16,024 (16%) eventually received a non-custodial sentence (Ministry of Justice, 2014e: Table 1.1). The average time spent in custody by remand prisoners awaiting trial and/or sentence has been estimated to be nine weeks (House of Commons, 2013).

Costs in Brief

Insofar as costs are concerned, the average cost of a prison place for the financial year 2012-13 was £36,808 excluding expenditure met by other government departments such as healthcare and education (Ministry of Justice 2013c: Table 1). The National Offender Management Service (NOMS), as the largest single spending area of the Ministry of Justice, had a budget of £4 billion, or two-fifths of the entire Ministry of Justice allocation (Whitehead, 2014; Prison Reform Trust, 2014: 5).

Post-Release Re-Offending

Reliable statistical evidence on recidivism is difficult to compile to standards of confidence normally associated with rigorous criminological research. Such is particularly the case where offenders released from prison following short terms of custody are not subject to post-sentence supervision.[7] Though modern computer-based data retrieval systems are routinely used within and between criminal justice agencies (police, courts, prison and probation services), these rely upon the quality of information input compatibility and data recording protocols over periods of years in duration.

Such data as are available suggest that 45.2% of adults are reconvicted within one year of being released, and that for those serving sentences of less than twelve months this rate rises to 57.5% – an increase of 3.2% since 2000 (Ministry of Justice, 2014f: Table 19a). Other studies that are not strictly comparable have indicated that 58% of young adults (18- to 20-year-olds) released from custody in the first quarter of 2008 re-offended with a year, and that 68.2% of juvenile offenders (10- to 17-year-olds) released in the twelve months ending September 2012 re-offended similarly (Prison Reform Trust, 2014: 29).

7 Here it will be noted that in England and Wales, early release from custody is governed by the provisions of the Criminal Justice Act 1991 under which those serving sentences of less than twelve months are automatically released having served one half of their sentence on automatic unconditional release (AUR) until their sentence expiry date.

There is also some evidence to indicate that among seriously recidivist adult offenders who have served more than eleven custodial sentences, rates of re-offending increase considerably to 68.7% of all adult offenders, and 75% of women offenders (Ministry of Justice, 2013d: Table 7a; and 2012b: Tables S5.26 and S5.28).

Implications of the Foregoing Analysis

From the brief survey of the existing state of prisons and prisoners in England and Wales provided above, it will have become evident to the reader that adoption of the retributive desert model as the basis of penal policies and practices has had a number of identifiable outcomes that, taken together, have served to make the criminal justice system largely unfit for any other purpose than that of incarceration. Leaving aside the traditional and historical antecedent influences that may have encouraged the development of such a situation over decades past, it is demonstrably the case that, since the mid-1990s, remedial measures that could have been set in place to reverse the trend of placing increasing and intolerable pressures on the agencies of criminal justice were either politically overlooked or deliberately ignored.

Two very perceptive analyses of this 'sleepwalking into chaos' development over the past two decades were provided by eminently well-qualified and respected observers of the criminal justice system as the new century dawned:

> For 40 years or more, it has not been possible to align sentencing policy with the capacity of the penal system in any way that the judiciary will accept. In crude terms, the courts have usually overfilled whatever prison capacity has been available, and whenever new types of non-custodial penalties have been provided to relieve pressure on the prisons, they have largely been used to punish people who would previously have received a more lenient disposal. (Dunbar & Langdon, 1998: 59)

And,

> Nonetheless, the bottom line is that current policies, political rhetoric and punishment patterns are as they are because politicians, however motivated, wished it so. ... Looking on the bright side, that conclusion means that directions can change if politicians wish it so. Looking on the dark side, however, as the proposals in the White Paper and the Criminal Justice Bill testify,[8] the

8 Later, the Criminal Justice Act 2003.

> Labour government shows no signs of wishing to return to policies that are more moderate, substantive, humane and effective than those it has promoted since taking office. (Tonry, 2003: 6)

The former quotation is from Ian Dunbar and Andrew Langdon's *Tough Justice: Sentencing and Penal Policies in the 1990s* (1998). Ian Dunbar was a former Director of Inmate Administration and Andrew Langton a Director of Operational Policy in the Prison Service. The latter is from Michael Tonry's edited work *Confronting Crime: Crime Control Policy Under New Labour* (2003). Michael Tonry was (at the time of writing) Professor of Law and Public Policy and Director of the Institute of Criminology, University of Cambridge.

The simple truth of the present situation is that since those observations were made, matters have gone from bad to worse within the penal system of England and Wales. The penal policies inherited by the New Labour government that took office from the Conservatives in 1997, and which remained in power until 2010 when the Conservative/Liberal Democrat Coalition regained it, have differed little in substance other than becoming increasingly punitive. What was described as the 'penal crisis'of the mid- to late 1990s has become 'business as usual'. The average daily prison population has risen inexorably in the interim, and with increasing momentum since 2002 in particular.

Overcrowding in prisons, entirely caused by enforced resort to cell sharing in accommodation originally designed for single occupancy, borders on inhumane practice but has other dysfunctional effects. For while additional numbers of inmates can be housed – albeit in cramped and unsatisfactory conditions – stresses are placed upon the supervisory and logistical functions that should otherwise permit constructive and purposeful regimes to operate.[9] From 2013 to 14 almost twenty thousand (23%) of prisoners were held in such conditions throughout the prisons estate (House of Commons, 2014).

Prison overcrowding is caused by the operational outcomes of court sentencing policies and practices. Here it is clear that increasing use has been made of immediate custody as a punishment over the past decade, of short periods of imprisonment in preference to community penalties, and that average sentence lengths have increased, including those imposed on life sentence prisoners. In addition, resort to the use of indeterminate sentences such as the ISPP and discretionary life sentences, and the recent legislation for the EDS described earlier have resulted in more and more people being held in prisons for increasing periods of time. Failure by the authorities[10] to operate the tariff-based concept

9 This pressure bears upon catering, healthcare, educational, recreational and inmate employment provisions designed to maintain purposeful regimes for the number of inmates for which the establishments were taken into use. It also makes the routine supervisory tasks of prison staff more difficult to complete to acceptable standards, while leading also to longer periods of each day spent by prisoners in cells with no constructive activities to keep them occupied.

10 And in particular, the Parole Board and Ministry of Justice departments responsible for sentence review and tariff considerations of ISPP, ESPP and discretionary life-sentenced prisoners.

of the ISPP and extended sentence for public protection (ESPP) provisions in a satisfactory manner served merely to exacerbate an already overstretched accommodation situation.

The size of the remand population in prison custody fluctuates with the ability of the courts to conduct trials without undue delay. The recent increase in this population has been largely due to such delays, increased use of remand in custody, and a risk-averse attitude disproportionate to the fact that some 27% of those remanded to await trial or sentence are either acquitted or do not eventually attract a custodial sentence.

High rates of reconviction of offenders within relatively short periods after release from prisons, and in particular those sentenced to short terms of prison custody, become a recurring feature of increased use of imprisonment. Given the circumstances in which overcrowded prisons are obliged to operate, it is only to be expected that little, if anything, can be done to address the behavioural and other deficits of short-sentenced prisoners who, effectively, 'clog up' the already depleted regimes of prison establishments. The additional fact that on release those sentenced to less than twelve months receive no post-release supervision within the community increases the likelihood of recidivism. It becomes only logical to question whether it is not ultimately counterproductive in the circumstances to send them to prison in the first place.

These are the factual implications of adopting the retributive desert model of criminal punishment as the core ingredient of criminal justice policies. There are, however, other real but less measurable outcomes associated with such policies. In the first place, prisons are, by their very nature, closed environments within which criminality is an endemic fact of life. Survival, for those imprisoned, depends upon coming to terms with the unwritten rules of the inmate subculture which can be predatory, violent and devious, and within which the weak become targets for exploitation by the strong, no matter how vigilant the supervisory efforts of correctional staff may be.

Prisons are also places within which criminality can be increased through the enforced association of individuals, many with extensive background experiences of offending, and some for whom their criminal behaviour has become a preferred lifestyle in which periods of time spent in custody are merely an interruption. The longer the time spent in such conditions, the greater the risk that the offender will emerge from the prison experience damaged to some extent – either physically or psychologically – and probably with an enhanced level of criminality.

There are also collateral effects of imprisonment upon the families and dependents of prisoners that can be extensive in terms of material deprivation and family breakdown. In England and Wales it has been estimated that some 200,000 children had a parent in prison at some point in 2009 (Ministry of Justice, 2012c), and that more than 17,240 children were separated from their mother by imprisonment in 2010 (Office for National Statistics, 2011).

During the first five years of this new millennium, a number of influential reports were produced, each of which indicated the research evidence to support the contention that short prison sentences (of up to twelve months duration) were largely ineffective in reducing recidivism (Home Office, 2001; Home Office, 2002; Esmeé Fairbairn Foundation, 2004a and 2004b; and see Cornwell, 2007: 145-156).[11] In spite of these conclusions, and the admission in the White Paper *Justice for All* that such sentences were even likely to encourage re-offending (Home Office, 2002: 92 and 102), the advice went largely unheeded by successive home secretaries[12] and their policy advisers anxious to be seen to pursue 'tough on crime' agendas.

Where from Here?

As the title of this chapter has suggested, the criminal justice systems of England and Wales, and of a number of other countries similarly placed, stand at a crossroads where strategic political choices must ultimately be made. It is, of course, a relatively simple matter to scapegoat politicians on the basis that 'criminal justice policies are as they are because politicians wished it so', as Michael Tonry pointed out. For while this may be true in theory, the pressures upon them to maintain the *status quo* are very considerable in terms of retaining electoral credibility.

But is maintenance of the *status quo* either desirable or unavoidable? A cursory glance at the corresponding imprisonment rates of the neighbouring countries of Western Europe may provide an interesting basis for comparison as the following table indicates.

11 These reports were made under the chairmanship of distinguished authors after which they became named. Home Office, 2001, The 'Halliday Report'; Esmeé Fairbairn Foundation, 2004a., The 'Coulsfield Report'; and 2004b., 'The Linklater Report'. Home Office (2002) was a White Paper, '*Justice for All*', CM 5563, London: HMSO, 2002..

12 And in 2007 and onwards Ministers of Justice on the formation of that Ministry.

Table 5.1 Imprisonment Rates Western Europe per 100,000 of Population

Nation	Rate *per* 100,000 population
England & Wales	148
Scotland	146
Spain	144
Portugal	138
Belgium	108
France	103
N. Ireland	101
Italy	100
Austria	98
Rep. Ireland	89
Switzerland	87
Netherlands	82
Germany	78
Denmark	73
Norway	72
Sweden	60
Finland	58

Sources: Wikipedia.org updated 11 December 2014 and ICPS, World Prison Brief 2014, London: ICPS
See: http://en.wikipedia.org/wiki/List_of_Countries_by_incarceration_rate (Accessed 8 January 2015) and also see, www.prisonstudies.org/world-prison-brief (Accessed 9 January 2015).

If the above rates were to be plotted graphically, the median rate of incarceration *per* 100,000 of population throughout the 17 countries listed would lie at 98.06. This value, coincidentally, lies exactly at the mid-point of the table. However, if the four countries that use imprisonment the most were to be excluded from the calculation, the median rate would fall significantly to 85.30 over the thirteen remaining countries.

The purpose of including the table at this stage of the discussion is to suggest that the countries of Western Europe as democracies display a wide variation is the extent to which imprisonment is used. At the upper extreme, those countries that comprise the United Kingdom all appear at rates considerably above the median. By way of contrast, the countries comprising the Scandinavian group of countries all occupy the lowest quartile at rates significantly below the median, leaving the remainder clustered around the median level itself. It is within the Scandinavian tradition that deliberate strategic policy decisions have been made and maintained to reduce the use of imprisonment to the minimum necessary. The British tradition is to ignore the benefits of doing so in pursuit of retributive policies placing no limits upon prison use, in spite of considerable research-based evidence that to do so is largely counterproductive in reducing recidivist crime.

The situation described above inevitably leads to some stark conclusions about the ultimate sustainability of the British approach to criminal justice at present and in the longer term. The evidence of the past decade is of an ever-upward spiralling of custodial sentencing which, if not checked and reversed, must lead to increasing demand for additional prison places, more and larger prisons, unacceptable costs and additional levels of post-sentence re-offending. And for as long as demand continues to outstrip the conditions in which prisons can serve the purposes of crime reduction, the prisons will remain overcrowded and unfit for any purpose other than incarceration for public protection. It is, ultimately, an inescapable fact that for as long as desert of punishment remains locked into its present deontological and taken-for-granted retributive justification, the situation cannot and will not change.

Resolution of these seemingly intractable problems clearly lies in a new strategic approach based upon an evidently consequentialist construction of desert in a utilitarian mode of conception: one in which the ends justify the means rather than *vice versa*. This implies a political willingness to reconceive a criminal justice system specifically focused on crime reduction rather than on incapacitation, on change-facilitative measures rather than on punitive reaction, on inclusion rather than exclusion, and on social involvement in justice rather than justice operated in isolation from community participation. Such a paradigm shift requires a social consensus inspired by political leadership of the highest quality and determination, dedicated to crime reduction rather than an ephemeral preoccupation with crime control and risk management.

In the next two chapters we shall consider the nature of an alternative strategy, how a social consensus for more enlightened justice might be constructed, and how some of the more resistant attitudes to change might be persuaded of the necessity to cooperate in building that consensus. Every strategic model needs a widely endorsed strategic purpose, simply expressed and logically consistent in its construction. Without such a purpose the enterprise will lack the focus necessary for its fulfilment, and the driving impetus for its achievement. It is, therefore, necessary to describe the nature of a revised criminal justice strategy and its implications for change first. These are considered in Chapter 6.

Part 2
Desert and Its Operational Implications

6 A Reparative Desert Strategy

Setting the Scene

This chapter is predicated upon the premise that criminal justice systems are designed to facilitate crime reduction; that this is essentially an enterprise focused on the future; and that, therefore, criminal punishment as a means of achieving crime reduction must have a primarily prospective purpose. This does not deny the fact that one element of the punitive process is also necessarily retributive and therefore retrospective,[1] but this is not (or should not be) the primary purpose of criminal justice.

This premise is based on the assumption that no human society is, or ever has been free of crime, but that reduction of crime to within socially tolerable limits is a desirable enterprise in the common interest of peaceful and harmonious co-existence, and the preservation of individual and collective liberties. It is further implicit within the premise that the commission of crime can never be completely *controlled* within free societies, but it can be *reduced* by changing wrongful patterns of behaviour into law-abiding ones, and that this is the ultimate purpose of criminal law and of justice.

Writing almost exactly fifty years ago, Wolfgang Friedmann summed up the nature of the criminal law in the following terms:

> The state of the criminal law continues to be as it should – a decisive reflection of the social consciousness of a society. What kind of conduct an organised community considers at a given time sufficiently condemnable to impose official sanctions, impairing the life, liberty, or property of the offender, is a barometer of the moral and social thinking of a community. Hence, the criminal law is particularly sensitive to changes in social structure and social thinking. (Friedmann, 1964, quoting Wechsler, 1955: 374, cited in Prins, 1982: 3)

The extent to which such a statement remains rather more aspirational than rational in the contemporary situation of criminal justice in Britain is open to debate. Laws, and in particular criminal laws, are enacted by parliament, and hence have legality even though they frequently reflect the ideological agenda of the dominant political majority. Fried-

1 Since legal punishment is imposed only upon those found guilty of an offence committed in the past, and not upon those who are innocent of committing any offence, or who might be deemed likely to do so in the future. Certain measures taken by governments to prevent crime being committed in the future may be restrictive of individual or collective civil liberties, but do not constitute criminal punishment *per se* even though these may be burdensome to some or another extent.

mann's analysis evidently assumes a significant level of informed community involvement, consultation and consensus in the law-making process,[2] augmented by rigorous consideration of the moral and social implications of the law's implementation.

The point is of importance for this work and at this stage because discussion of a reparative desert strategy involves consideration of a different approach to criminal justice from that of the traditional retributive model previously described. What will be proposed here is a conception of justice based upon restorative justice principles, and which can only be achieved in practice through a genuine political and professional consensus that it would deliver better justice to all the legitimate stakeholders in the justice process – the state, offenders, victims and communities.

Contrasted Models of Desert

It will be recalled from Chapter 4 that the two models of justice under discussion – the retributive desert and the reparative desert models – though entirely different in conception, originated from a situation of competing ethical values. The former model would insist that crime or wrongdoing axiomatically deserves the response of punishment in order that the law should be upheld and be seen to be upheld, and that the outcomes of that process are of secondary importance to the evident justice of the punishment and its manifest imposition. The latter model proposes that, while acknowledging the harm caused by crime, the outcomes of the justice process are of greater ethical and social importance than the imposition of punishment entirely for its own sake, however that process is justified.

In a consequentialist (or utilitarian) sense, the second of these models goes considerably further. It expresses the principle that those harmed by crime deserve some form of reparation for the distress caused to them, and that it is primarily the responsibility of the offender to take account of this, accept guilt for his actions, show remorse, and make apology and reparation where this is possible and acceptable.[3] In such a manner, those harmed by crime are to some extent vindicated, those who cause the harm have a means by which they may be restored to full citizenship, and disturbance caused within communities where crime is committed is in some degree reduced. Proponents of such a model

2 The term 'community' implied here is problematic. Opinion forming among the general public is to a greater extent dominated by the editorial policies of the mass media (press and television) and the burgeoning social media than was the case in the 1960s. By 'community' in this context, is also implied those agencies and organisations (both governmental and non-governmental) with a legitimate claim to be consulted on an evidential basis as parties to policy making and/or implementation. It is also the case that in the 1960s greater governmental and political attention was paid to consultation with academic and professional bodies in the process of policy making than is the practice now.

3 Subject, obviously, to certain necessary safeguards to protect the wellbeing and privacy of victims, ensuring that they are not further traumatised or revictimised in any reconciliation process in which their participation must be entirely voluntary.

would insist that it is in all respects preferable to the retributive model which makes no such demands upon offenders, while at the same time being largely unconcerned about the effects of crime upon its victims.[4]

Now, it might be supposed that these two models of desert are entirely mutually exclusive, but that is far from being a claim made in this work, and this issue is discussed in some detail in the next chapter. More important for the present is the need to establish the moral and ethical credentials of a reparative model of desert since that might also make it possible to resolve a number of the evident shortcomings within the retributive model outlined in the previous chapter to be resolved to a greater or lesser extent.

In some respects, the reparative desert model reflects an element of what was formerly described as the rehabilitative ethic widely adopted until its demise in the 1970s as described earlier. Its purposes do, however, range beyond the rehabilitation of offenders which might still be achieved through reparation, and incorporate into penological thinking and action a deliberate focus upon victim inclusiveness. It is thus a dual purpose model that seeks to 'put wrongs right' through evident consideration of the needs of victims, while at the same time affording offenders the means of social restoration, through the making of apology and reparation, to full community status.[5] These purposes are entirely consistent with the principles of restorative justice as originally articulated by Albert Eglash (1977) and Howard Zehr (1990 and 2002),[6] and many others since. This stated, the reparative desert model is proposed as one that sits (or has the potential to sit) as a complementary strategy for crime reduction *alongside* its retributive counterpart. The reasons for this claim require further explanation which follows.

The Dual Desert Paradigm

As we have noted previously, far too many offenders found guilty of offences in the medium to less serious extents of gravity are sentenced to short prison sentences in England and Wales and elsewhere. Their presence in prisons contributes significantly to the endemic overcrowding problem, and their offences could, in other circumstances, be dealt with by

4 Other, perhaps, than to the extent that these effects reflect the gravity of the crime. Such is not to suggest that judges and other legal officials in courts are callous or indifferent towards crime victims, but rather that the primary purpose of the criminal courts is to bring the guilty to justice, and that within the Anglo-Saxon tradition of justice administration, issues of compensation are largely the task of the civil courts to resolve.

5 It will here be evident that, within this concept, the term 'restoration' is preferred to that of 'rehabilitation' to avoid the valid criticisms of the former rehabilitative ethic as a *quasi*-medical model of 'curing' intervention through cognitive behavioural and other therapy-based programmes. Though such programmes have a place in treating addictions and psychiatric disorders, many offenders need access to educational and life skills opportunities to a greater extent than psychological interventions.

6 Even though it will be recalled that originally Zehr considered restorative justice and retributive justice to be antithetical (1990), but later modified this view (2002).

sanctions of a non-custodial nature. On the other hand, those who commit more serious offences of a violent or predatory nature present a level of public risk that may make terms of imprisonment unavoidable. The potential of prisons to deal effectively with such offenders in terms of risk reduction is considerably affected by the same overcrowding situation.

Many less serious offenders, when confronted with the harm caused by their offences to victims are genuinely ashamed of their actions and are prepared to make amends for these given an opportunity to do so. The circumstances leading to their offences may vary considerably, and many of them would also wish to avoid re-offending given some assistance to do so. These offenders may be said to deserve the opportunity to make apology and reparation while receiving the necessary assistance through counselling, addressing the causes of their offending, or life skills training. If such is the case, sending them to prison is entirely counterproductive and seriously wasteful of expensive resources.

Dealing with such people within the community requires a correctional services structure specifically designed to deliver the reparative strategy, and within which there is also a considerable level of community involvement. Such has historically been the province of National Probation Service or similar government organisations which have lacked the role definition, structure and resources to meet such a commitment. This to a considerable extent also explains why overuse has been made of short-term custodial sentencing. It may also be suggested that part of the desert debate arises because such a structure is a matter of genuine social need that has, hitherto, been neglected or under-resourced since short-term imprisonment became perceived as a readily available alternative.

The same cannot be said of serious offenders, many of whom are relatively remorseless and present an obvious public risk, and for whom lengthier periods of imprisonment are necessary to reflect the gravity of their crimes. However, there comes a point in time at which even such prisoners reach the period approaching their release, and when serious consideration has to be given to preparing them for their return to their communities. These are people who may have been out of touch with community life for some years, and/or who may have become heavily institutionalised by that experience.[7] Their return to normal community life therefore requires a stage-by-stage preparation under the supervision of professionals trained to advise and assist them until they are capable of surviving independently. This is yet another facet of desert which is much understated, and yet which flows directly from the operational effects of the retributive desert model.

7 The term 'institutionalisation' is used to describe the way in which long-term inmates of prisons and other residential institutions become so dependent upon the routines and rules under which they are confined as to lose their sense of self-regulation and independence. Some become even fearful of their ability to survive and function effectively within the wider community, many having lost family and friendship contacts, and having no available place of domicile due to the duration of their absence from community life.

From what has been suggested albeit briefly here, it will be evident that considerations of desert within criminal justice are infinitely more complex than the narrow conception of retributive justice that derives from the fact of an offence against the law having been committed, the perpetrator convicted, and therefore punishment administered – however appropriately or inappropriately. In whatever manner these forms of desert are classified (*i.e.* positive and negative, deontological or consequentialist, or otherwise), each may be 'merited' in differing circumstances.[8]

Desert in its relationship with victims of crime has also been seen to flow from the involuntary nature of the distress or suffering of those harmed by offending. Some victims of violent or sexual crime are severely traumatised by their experiences on a short- or long-term basis, and most particularly when physical injury or psychological damage is severe and of lengthy duration. Yet the criminal law, with its narrow focus upon guilt and punishment, remains curiously distanced from the wider and merited needs of victims to be considered, vindicated and compensated.[9]

From the foregoing discussion it will be evident that the essential nature of desert in its various forms does not fit exclusively with either a retributive desert theory or its reparative desert counterpart: nor does it make them mutually exclusive, but rather to a significant extent complementary. It is to the implications of this situation that the remaining part of this chapter is devoted.

Fitting Desert into an Operational Framework

The premise adopted at the start of this chapter suggested the need for a forward-looking interpretation of desert designed to promote crime reduction as opposed to crime control as an operational *modus operandi*. The nature of offenders and their offences, combined with the legitimate needs of victims and communities discussed in the previous section, reinforce such a contention. This in turn means that, in terms of the operational delivery of appropriate justice, penal systems of the future must accommodate these dimensional requirements while still fulfilling the primary purpose of crime reduction. In order to do so, prisons have to be freed of the scourge of overcrowding and be able to deliver full and purposeful regimes; community corrections have to be expanded and made capable of providing reparative outcomes combined with life skills enhancement and counselling; and communities have to become actively involved as stakeholders in the crime reduction

8 'Merited' as intended here is in the sense of being appropriate, fair and just in the different circumstances considered.

9 Other, that is, than in the status of victims as prosecution witnesses in criminal trials, and in consideration of victim impact statements (VISs) or victim personal statements (VPSs) if submitted, prior to deliberation of sentences. Issues of compensation or reparation remain largely the province of the civil law and courts as previously noted.

strategy. Overarching all of these essential requirements, the systemic structure of correctional services has to become unified and integrated as the dynamic motive driving force of a restructured penal system.

Implicit within such an agenda for change lies the challenge of creating a consensus between all the parties with a legitimate interest in the processes of criminal justice that the restructuring is not only long overdue, but also that it is a moral, economic, and operational imperative if the strategy of crime reduction is to be achieved. These interested parties include (and involve) politicians, policymakers, the judiciary, academics, penal system professionals,[10] police services, court officials, the media and ultimately the public in a consultation process with the common purpose of 'doing justice better'.

Accommodating both the reparative and the retributive desert models in a complementary (or side-by-side) manner within a single penal policy strategy will require a bifurcated system of criminal justice which requires some explanation at this stage of the discussion. The term 'bifurcation' implies a twin-track approach to dealing with offenders within a single and unified correctional structure combining both custodial and community-based sentencing provision and administration. I have indicated the nature of such a structure in some detail in a previous work (Cornwell, 2009: 153-155 and *passim*; 2010: 7-20)[11] and in consequence will summarise the argument for bifurcation more briefly here.

The essential features of a bifurcated criminal justice system are threefold. First, to provide separate custodial facilities that are appropriate for delivery of reparative regimes for those offenders deemed suitable and willing to participate in them. Second, to provide 'traditional' regimes for long-term and less amenable offenders in conditions of appropriate security and with purposeful activity. Third, to bridge the present 'custody/community divide' between sentencing provisions within a unified correctional services structure that delivers seamless transitional progression and community sanctions with an evident 'penal bite'.[12]

As to the first of these features, and assuming that resort to short-term sentences of imprisonment[13] were to be largely dispensed with as has been widely recommended, it would be appropriate to establish a network of reparative prisons for those offenders considered to be both willing and behaviourally suitable to work to make reparation to

---

10 Including the prison and probation services, the Parole Board and the providers of court and national prisoner movement and escorting services.

11 The latter reference is to an article published in the Dutch/Flemish Journal of Restorative Justice *Tijdschrift voor Herstelrecht*, 2010 (10) on pp. 7-20. An English language translation of this article can be made available upon request to the author or the publishers of this work.

12 The term 'penal bite' implied here is intended to describe community sanctions with a demanding and measurable punitive content in which public confidence can become assured.

13 Of up to twelve months imprisonment or less of which only one half is spent in prison custody and the remainder on unconditional release without supervision in the community. But here see Note 14 below.

victims of crime, and whose sentences were of relatively limited duration.[14] Such prisons could be have less security since it might be envisaged that towards the latter part of reparative sentences inmates might spend a period of time on day release licence working within the local community. It would therefore be appropriate for such prisons to be designed with integral hostel-type accommodation to which those 'working out' would return each evening.

In relation to the second feature of a bifurcated system, 'traditional' prisons would remain necessary – but freed from overcrowding to enable positive and purposeful regimes to function effectively. It might be considered possible for some inmates serving longer fixed sentences and approaching their scheduled release dates to become eligible (if considered suitable) for transfer to reparative prisons for the final custodial period of a sentence. Such a period would coincide with that period of sentence presently served either in custody or on discretionary conditional release (DCR) under present arrangements in England and Wales.[15] The conditions governing life sentences and the release of such prisoners from custody would remain as at present.

The third feature mentioned above is more problematic. At the present time there is a clear demarcation between the work of the prison and probation services, both of which are elements of the NOMS headed by a Director General of Criminal justice and Offender Management. The only bridge between the operational roles of the two services is the presence of probation officers seconded to undertake casework in prisons, and the offender management model developed by the National Probation Service within which a designated manager takes overall responsibility for each offender sentenced to imprisonment or a community penalty throughout the period of the sentence (see: Gibson, 2009: 115).

Though the core work of the two services is evidently different in nature and each has its own distinctive historical and operational ethos, there are areas of overlap in relation to the release of prisoners either temporarily or under licence supervision conditions within the community. A marked decrease in the use of short custodial sentences would inevitably result in an increase in the use of community sanctions. Moreover, both a reparative desert model and a bifurcated custodial system would envisage an increase in the use of temporary

14 Possibly of up to four years imprisonment which, under current rules (Criminal Justice Act 1991) in England and Wales, require up to half of the sentence period to be spent in prison custody, one quarter on automatic conditional release (ACR) on licence under supervision, and the final quarter on automatic unconditional release (AUR). However, as Cavadino and Dignan (1997: 190-2) have pointed out, the term 'unconditional' is something of a misnomer as the unexpired portion of the sentence is held in suspense, and may be re-activated if a new offence is committed and convicted before the end of the original term, or sentence expiry date (SED).

15 Under present CJA 1991 arrangements, prisoners serving fixed-term (determinate) sentences of four years or more spend one half of the sentence period in prison custody, a period spanning the one half to two-thirds point of the sentence either in custody or on discretionary conditional release (DCR), a further period up to the three-quarters point of sentence on ACR (see Note 14 above), and the final quarter of the sentence period under AUR conditions.

release of prisoners from reparative prisons to work in the community as a deliberate pre-release strategy.

Given the necessary expansion of community sanctions, and for reasons of assuring public confidence in the supervision of those offenders so sentenced or released from prisons to work in the community, a stronger relationship between the two services would become necessary. In ideal circumstances this would suggest the need for a unified correctional services structure within which both prison and probation professionals might work together in a more seamless manner. In view of the historical differences of professional ethos between the two services, however, such a suggestion may be greeted with considerable reluctance in the process of consensus building described earlier, and in greater detail in Chapter 7. It would certainly require determined leadership at every managerial level to become a reality, though the long-term advantages of such a restructuring would be considerable.

Reparative Desert as the Focus for Change

In the course of this and previous chapters, a number of important issues emerging from considerations of desert have been explored. Some of these are philosophical or conceptual in nature; others are operational aspects of criminal justice delivery. Central to the entire discussion is the contention that a concept of reparative desert is an essential component of criminal punishment philosophy which has been considerably overlooked or understated hitherto, and that its beneficial potential has historically been overshadowed by preoccupation with retributive desert both in theory and in practice.

There remains no doubt that the retributive desert model has enjoyed considerable political appeal since it has made it possible for politicians and the media to articulate a 'war on crime' concept of punitive policy making since the demise of the rehabilitative ethic. Such a concept has a certain resonance with a public consciousness conditioned by media reporting to believe that the risk to the average citizen of becoming a victim of crime is far greater than can be shown statistically to be the case. Allied to this belief has occurred an extensive 'demonisation' of sexual offenders in general, and of those accused of child molestation or abuse in particular.

The reparative model of desert stems to a considerable extent from the concept of restorative justice which has gained increasing acceptance among academics and criminal justice practitioners since the mid-1990s. Its particular philosophical strength lies in its victim inclusiveness that is significantly neglected by the retributive model. Though successive governments in Britain have expressed a superficial interest in expanding the use of restorative practices within criminal justice, the 'tough on crime' *mantra* with its electoral appeal for politicians has to date confined interest in restorative justice within the marginal waters of mainstream justice legislation.

Perhaps the most inexplicable feature of the criminal justice situation in Britain and some other Western European countries is an endemic ambivalence within politics and judicial behaviour in relation to the use of imprisonment. An ever-increasing prison population places an immense fiscal burden upon limited national resources, and is yet avoidable. Repeated government exhortations to an independent judiciary to make the use of custody a practice of last resort have self-evidently been largely ignored, while throughout the past two decades successive governments have enacted ever more draconian criminal justice legislation that has encouraged increased and lengthier use of prison custody. The outcomes of this political duplicity have been made evident in this work.

Development of a reparative ethos within criminal justice could, if deliberately adopted, provide the focus and the inspiration for long overdue reform of criminal justice delivery in many countries saddled with the burden of excessive penal costs. To achieve this transformation requires a social consensus that is achievable, but which requires inspired political leadership. In the chapter which follows, we shall explore how such a consensus might be created as it has been achieved elsewhere, and assess the social benefits that could accrue from such reform.

There also remain a number of unanswered questions that relate to the way in which a reparative desert model could be made operational in practice. These chiefly concern the types of offender that might be deemed suitable for mediated interventions, who would be responsible for instigating and conducting the mediation process, how true remorse expressed by offenders can be assessed, and whether certain categories of offences should be excluded from or included within the scope of mediation processes. Consideration also has to be given to the safeguarding of victims willing to enter into mediation from exploitation, how the outcomes of mediation should be conveyed to courts, and whether a code of conduct would be necessary to which it would be mandatory for mediators to adhere. These and related issues are addressed further in Chapter 8.[16]

Before doing so, however, and because the desired reforms cannot be envisaged in the absence of a significant consensus to achieve such change, it becomes essential to indicate how such a political and social consensus might be arrived at in practice. It is to this potentially critical process that the focus of attention is directed in Chapter 7.

16 I am grateful to my colleague Professor John Blad of Erasmus University, Rotterdam, the Netherlands, for his helpful and constructive comments on these issues in correspondence arising out of his review of *Mercy: A Restorative Philosophy*, (Cornwell, 2014a) in Blad, 2015: 68-73.

7 Consensus Building for Reform

Some General Observations

In the process of considering any situation in which a significant change of strategic direction has become necessary, the normal starting point is to understand why the existing state of affairs has become critical and its prolongation an unacceptable option. Some situations slide into crisis because, over time, managerial structures and their leadership become complacent and warning signs are ignored. Others in which corrective action is needed are subject to external pressures that are not within the power of an organisation to change or reduce, and thus a culture of 'helplessness' becomes endemic. In yet other situations organisations are tempted to adopt short-term fix measures of relief that address the symptoms rather than the causes of impending crises, and in the hope that the causal factors will change and make significant change avoidable as a long-term strategy.

Every crisis develops in a manner and in circumstances that are unique to the organisations in which it occurs, thus each such event requires countermeasures that specifically address its own causes and effects. There is frequently a temptation to import an 'off-the-shelf' solution based on solutions applied to apparently similar situations elsewhere as a means of applying a quick fix to the problem, and this normally fails to remedy satisfactorily the issues at hand.

In the specific instance of the penal crisis in England and Wales which has developed and deepened over the two decades past, a number of quick fixes have been attempted but the core of the problem has remained the same: too many prisoners, too many prisons, and too many re-offenders. Insofar as prisoners are concerned, an excessive number of them are sentenced to short terms of custody, and many others are serving sentences for longer than are necessary[1] and in conditions that are not conducive to changing offending behaviour. The response to the problem of too many prisoners has been to increase the number of prison places by resort to expanding or overcrowding existing prisons, and continuing to build even more and larger ones[2] rather than making lesser use of custodial sentences.

---

1 And of an indeterminate or extended nature imposed on the basis of public protection rather than entirely on the seriousness of the offences committed.

2 Although seventeen older and relatively small prisons have been closed since 2010, two new and larger prisons were opened in 2012, four more are being expanded by building additional accommodation, and work to develop a new 2,100 place prison is under way, with a further one of similar size under consideration. Twenty-nine prisons now hold over 1,000 inmates compared with only twelve in 2004-5 (Prison Reform Trust, 2014: 18). Postscript: In fact at the time of writing the number of prisons closed has risen to eighteen with the decision to close HMP Blantyre House made in January 2015.

The issue of high re-offending rates following periods of custody has been discussed earlier in this work. It is clearly evident that short prison sentences do not reduce recidivism and probably increase it. Overcrowding in prisons places significant pressures on the effectiveness of regime delivery,[3] and strictly limits those efforts that can be made to address offending behaviour within the custodial setting.

Returning briefly to the first paragraph of this chapter, it has been clearly established that the continuing crisis – which has almost ceased to be regarded as such in the penal system of England and Wales – shows features of all three of the causal factors mentioned. Warning signs have been ignored by successive governments since the mid-1990s; the Prison Service and National Probation Service have been subjected to an overload situation beyond the power of either to control; and the short-term 'fixes' applied to the Prison Service in terms of providing additional capacity have been both inadequate and ineffective. To make matters even worse, enactment of legislation such as the Criminal Justice Act 2003 and the Legal Aid, Sentencing and Punishment of Offenders Act 2012 reflects a deliberate attempt to make sentencing more punitive, and failure to control the sentencing behaviour of the courts has resulted in a continuous escalation of the prison population.

It is within this scenario that the urgent need for significant change has arisen, and has also been intensified by the imposition of spending reductions upon the agencies of the penal system. This is their contribution towards the government's agenda since 2010 to reduce the overall national budget deficit. Between 2011/12 and 2013/14 the National Offender Management Service has delivered £263m in spending reductions against a target of £274m, and is scheduled to deliver a further £149m in 2014/15 (National Offender Management Service, 2014 *passim*). These reductions and efficiency savings have to be viewed against the continuing trend since 2013 of the Prison Service operating above published population projections which, by April 2014, were 300 above the high projection and 1,300 above the medium projection (Ministry of Justice, 2014g; Prison Reform Trust, 2014: 20).

This is the backdrop against which a consensus for change has become necessary, and it is to a discussion of who must be involved in that consensus and why that the remaining sections of this chapter are devoted. The discussion will focus upon two distinctive clusters of organisations within the criminal justice system of England and Wales which might be described as interested parties within this consensus. It will, however, be seen that these clusters overlap to a considerable extent within the processes of justice administration. Viewed in its entirety, the criminal justice system described here is a historically complex

3 This is primarily a logistical problem since prisons are designed and equipped to deal with particular levels of occupancy in delivery of skill-enhancing employment, education and recreational programmes on the one hand, and medical, catering and visitation facilities on the other. When these establishments are expanded by adding cell accommodation, the increased level of occupancy leads to an overstretch of the logistical resources, and to a reduction in the hours that can be spent by inmates in a purposeful manner.

amalgam of government and other agencies, the nature of whose relationships may seem to readers from other countries to be obscure, if not even in some respects somewhat illogical. It is, therefore, in an attempt to make explanation of this situation more understandable that this approach has been devised.

Cluster 1 – The Key Strategic Institutions

It may surprise some readers of this work to know that, unlike in most European countries, there was no Ministry of Justice in the United Kingdom until May 2007. Until that year many of the routine functions of the criminal justice system fell within the remit of the Home Office which, even after 2007, retains responsibility for, *inter alia*, policing, border control and immigration matters. From May 2007, the newly created Ministry of Justice, headed by the Secretary of State for Justice,[4] assumed responsibility for the former Department of Constitutional Affairs (DCA) which it replaced, and the NOMS previously formed in 2004, and comprising both the Prison Service and National Probation Service as its main constituent elements.[5]

As Figure 7.1 illustrates, at a national level – described here as the 'strategic' level – there is a complex of institutions all with a vested interest in the formulation of criminal justice policies and practices, the framing of legislation, and its outcomes in terms of justice delivery. The incumbent ruling political party (or parties) forming the government of the day has a dominant influence in framing criminal justice legislation in accordance with its own ideological tradition, though this may be somewhat modified in wider parliamentary debates with opposition parties in the enactment of legislative provisions. Parliament, in both its upper and lower houses in England and Wales, is therefore the ultimate authority for the enactment and enforcement of laws of a criminal justice nature.

4 More widely referred to as the Justice Secretary, and who also fulfils the historical role of the Lord Chancellor.

5 For a more detailed explanation of this development see Gibson, 2009: 108 and 115. For the sake of additional clarity within this work, these entities are described as 'correctional services' which is a term used worldwide, and more precisely describes the role performed within criminal justice systems.

Figure 7.1 The State Dimension

CLUSTER 1 – KEY STRATEGIC INSTITUTIONS

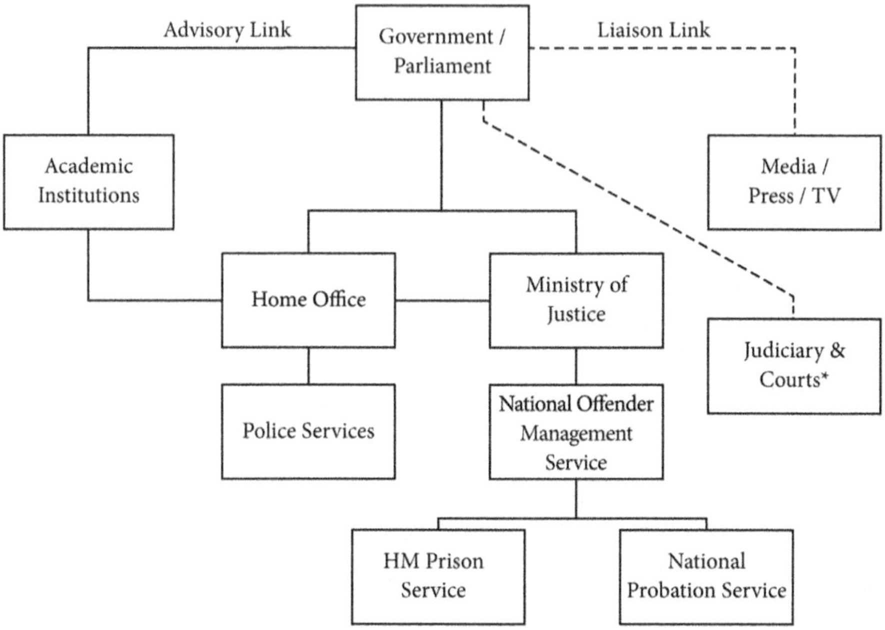

Note: * Includes Prosecution Services

Media Influence

It is difficult to state with any certainty the extent to which the mass media of television and newspaper reporting exert an influence upon political thinking and policy deliberation, but this influence is evidently considerable. The editorial policies of newspaper and television proprietors in shaping public opinion and urging government action in one or another direction is a major feature of political life in many countries – and particularly in relation to criminal justice policy making and legislation. It is in recognition of this fact that the presence and influence of the media are reflected in each of the cluster representations underlying this discussion.

What is clear, however, is that the media, as the most widespread and penetrative means of opinion forming within contemporary societies, exercise a largely uncontrollable influence upon public acceptance or rejection of putative criminal justice policies. Moreover, media studies and research have proved historically equivocal about the extent to which 'public opinion' is a measurable or even reliable concept for assessing or reflecting the true nature and extent of public tolerance in relation to criminal justice reform and other initiatives (see *e.g.* Heath, Fisher & Smith *et al.*, 2005: 54-59; Groves, 1987: 156-172; King, Murray, Salomon *et al.*, 2004: 191-207; Lynn, Gabler & Laaksonen, 2004; Schumann & Presser, 1981).[6]

As a consequence of these considerations, it is evident that the media have to be drawn into any consultative process designed to deliver significant penal reform such as that proposed in this work. Much would also depend upon the extent of the media's willingness to approach the task with an open-minded, balanced and constructive approach to the social necessity of the change required. It would also depend on their willingness to adopt an editorial stance that would encourage rather than hinder that process.

Academic Influence

Academic institutions have traditionally been a source of rigorous social science research and criminological expertise that has been increasingly underused by successive governments in Britain since the 1990s. The reasons for this situation are largely political in nature and require brief explanation here. During the post-World War II era and until the mid-1980s, it was customary practice for governments to commission universities with expertise in particular areas of research to undertake in-depth projects to evaluate policy and practice options to inform the process of legislative decision-making. Indeed, in 1957 the Home Office Research Unit (HORU) was established[7] to carry out in-house research and to 'extend assistance, advice', and allocate funds to universities to undertake projects associated with criminal justice policy and legislative research.

By the late 1970s, the HORU was increasingly reliant on its own research capability, and there was much less funding for university research. This situation developed because although the unit had the remit to decide which projects should be externally funded and supervised, the outcomes of the research could not be guaranteed to be consistent with the nature of the advice that ministers wished to receive and implement in terms of government policy initiatives.

---

6 Opinion polls differ widely in the manner in which they frame and conduct research, and are thus not strictly commensurable indicators of public opinion other than in a superficial sense. Much depends upon sample selection, extent and consistency in seeking and recording responses to questions which may also be framed differently by polling organisations investigating similar issues.

7 At Romney House, Marsham Street, London SW1, with suboffices in Manchester and Edinburgh. However, the first official funding of criminal justice-related research was authorised in the Criminal Justice Act 1948, which enabled the Home Secretary to allocate funding for research by universities and similar organisations as a means of informing government policy making and legislation. See: www.ncjrs.gov/pdffiles1/Digitization (Accessed 1 February 2015).

During the 1990s and subsequently, reliance by successive governments upon university-based research became infrequent, and academic expertise in the fields of criminology and penology was largely unsought, ignored or overlooked. Indeed, universities themselves increasingly sought and became reliant on funding from large private sector organisations and charities in order to undertake criminological research, and some even declined to apply for or undertake government funded projects due to the political constraints placed upon the methodological and outcome requirements - aspects that would significantly limit their academic independence.

Yet independent academic expertise and advice remain an invaluable aid to rational policy making that is available but undervalued as far as its rigorously reached analysis and commentary were concerned. It is for this reason that, if significant penal reform is as necessary and urgently required as this study reveals, then that expertise has to be brought back into the fold of government decision making and policy determination.

Judicial Influence

The British judiciary has a long-established tradition of independence from the executive and legislative functions of government derived from the concept of the separation of powers.[8] Thus although laws are enacted by parliament in its legislative role, and framed in policy form by the executive departments of government, in terms of the criminal laws the judiciary are required to implement the measures enacted, and have no specific powers to change the law.[9] Therefore, in relation to the multitude of offences in England and Wales in which the law provides for imprisonment as opposed to a community order to be used as a penalty in more serious instances, it requires that judicial discretion be exercised to decide upon relative seriousness (or gravity) as between offences falling within the same generic description.

In seeking the nature of the consensus for change envisaged here, lesser resort to the use of imprisonment would either have to be imposed upon the judiciary by statute,[10] or

8 A concept traceable back to Aristotle and the political divisions within the city states of Ancient Greece, and mirrored in the Roman Republic. In principle, the main components of government – executive, legislative and judiciary – should be able to operate independently without any one of them dominating the others or interfering in their areas of operation. The first significant explanation of the principle may be found in the political works of Montesquieu in eighteenth century France (1914). For a further explanation see: Stewart (2004).

9 This is, however, a moot point insofar as the concept of equitable justice implies an extent of interpretive discretion in pursuit of fairness, allowing the spirit of the law to override its literal meaning in instances unusual or unforeseen (see, *e.g.* Cornwell, 2014b: 28-9).

10 Such is to suggest in the framing of legislation strictly limiting the use of short custodial sentences as was achieved in Germany during the 1960s and 1970s (Wiegend, 2001 *passim*; Tonry & Frase, 2001; and see also Cornwell, 2007: 165).

adopted by sentencing officials as a matter of practice direction.[11] It would, however, be preferable if the judiciary could be persuaded of the necessity of using custody more sparingly, though such exhortations have proved largely ineffective hitherto. It seems, rather, to be the case that use of custody – where it is legislatively permitted – has been perceived by judges and magistrates as an 'unlimited option' since prisons in Britain, unlike those in a number of European countries, cannot refuse to accept offenders thus sentenced when already overcrowded or at full capacity.[12]

This leaves largely unresolved the important issue of to whom the judiciary are accountable in an operational sense since the changes in their structure brought about by the Constitutional Reform Act 2005. The Act established the new Supreme Court while at the same time removing the Lords of Appeal in Ordinary (aka Law Lords) from the House of Lords and changing the role of the Lord Chief Justice. The Act is applicable to all the courts of the United Kingdom, and thus falls beyond the remit of the Lord Chief Justice of England and Wales. The latter was retitled President of the Courts of England and Wales, the judicial function of which countries was transferred to a Judicial Executive Board headed by the President with the most senior judges as members.

An independent Judicial Appointments Commission was also established to recommend suitable candidates for appointment to the Justice Secretary and Lord Chancellor, along with a strengthening of the Judges Council that includes all levels and members of the judiciary including the magistracy. The Lord Chief Justice of England and Wales now represents the views of the judiciary to Parliament and ministers, but the issue and manner of ultimate accountability remains somewhat unspecified.[13] Here it should also be noted that in Britain, unlike a number of Western European countries, judges are not civil servants and thus are not subject to the civil service conditions of employment and remuneration. They are, in effect, appointed for life, and their conduct in office is subject to the scrutiny only of their peers as members of the Judicial Executive Board.

The Departments of State

Mention has been made earlier of both the Home Office and the Ministry of Justice which are chiefly involved in matters pertaining to the criminal justice system of England and

---

11 Practice directions are issued from time to time by the Lord Chief Justice of England and Wales in the form of instructions binding upon members of the judiciary in their implementation of court practices and procedures. For further explanation see: Gibson, 2009: 124.

12 Unlike their counterparts in Finland, the Netherlands, Denmark and Norway where statutory limitations have been placed upon the capacity of prisons operating at or in excess of full capacity (see: Lappi-Seppälä, 2001; Tak, 2001; Kyvsgaard, 2001; and Larsson, 2001 all quoted in Tonry, 2003: 212-3).

13 For a further explanation of these reforms see: http://judiciary.gov.uk/about-the-judiciary (Accessed 4 February 2015).

Wales. These two organisations will continue to feature prominently in subsequent discussion, and in particular in relation to the next cluster which deals with law enforcement to which we shall now turn.

Cluster 2 – The Law Enforcement Agencies

The strategic structure of law enforcement in England and Wales is shown diagrammatically in Figure 7.2 (overleaf) which indicates the complex of government agencies tasked with the various responsibilities that contribute to it. The formation of the Ministry of Justice in 2007 provoked significant organisational change within these agencies, while at the same time making certain others effectively redundant.[14] As part of the settling-down process following its formation, it became necessary to restructure the management of the Ministry of Justice under a number of directors general, the subsequent responsibilities of whom are explained in detail in Bryan Gibson's informative and helpful work *The New Ministry of Justice: An Introduction*, (2nd ed.), 2008, to which the reader seeking a more comprehensive account is referred.

The principal issue within this work, and in particular in relation to the task of building a consensus for change within the criminal justice structure, is the wide span of agencies within and outside the Ministry of Justice that retain a specific interest in, and focus upon, the processes of law enforcement and justice administration. As an instance of this situation, the police have a primary interest in the detection of crime and maintenance of public order by identifying, arresting and charging suspected offenders; prosecution officials are involved in bringing suspected offenders to justice having evaluated the evidence alleged against them; the Courts and Tribunals Service administers the functioning of the courts (both criminal and civil) and tribunals in which the judiciary (judges and magistrates) preside over trials or proceedings. The correctional (prison and probation) services are responsible for dealing with offenders who are tried and sentenced on either a custodial or a non-custodial basis. Some of these agencies, and the judiciary, function with primary responsibility and accountability to departments of state other than the Ministry of Justice.

14 Among which were notably the former Lord Chancellor's Department (LCD) and the Department for Constitutional Affairs (DCA).

Figure 7.2 Law Enforcement

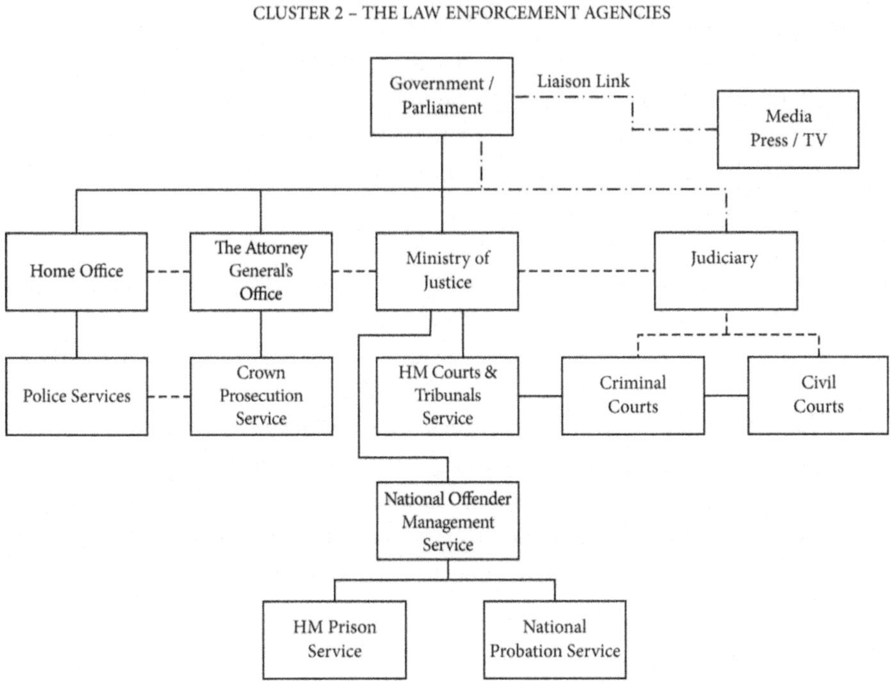

Even within the Ministry of Justice and its National Offender Management Service there exist significant historical and professional differences of ethos between the prison and probation services. These have hitherto defied and obstructed any notion of creating a unified correctional services structure that could operationally provide an almost seamless delivery of custodial and community sentencing outcomes, and the transition from one to the other within a bifurcated sentencing structure. Such a situation suggests the need for a primary consensus between these two services that both have complementary and overlapping roles within the process of justice delivery, rather than discrete and divisionary agendas and purposes that effectively preclude any concept of unification.

These difficulties and situations apart, it will be recalled that the purpose of this work is to propose a criminal justice structure that delivers to all its stakeholders the quality of justice that each deserves, and in which the public can be confident. At the heart of this structure lie the prison and probation services whose responsibility it is to deliver what should now be termed correctional services in a unified manner. It is therefore to a description of this structure that we now turn.

Towards a Consensus for Strategic Change

This chapter has indicated the need for a consensus among the stakeholders of criminal justice in relation to the need for strategic change in policies and practices in England and Wales to deliver better justice. Although the present structure discussed has been that which exists in these countries, the situation to be resolved is common to other countries in Western Europe and elsewhere: that of excessive penal populations that are neither justifiable nor affordable in contemporary societies.

In normal circumstances in which strategic organisational change is considered it might seem appropriate first to define the desired strategy before identifying the organisational components necessary to draw into a consensus to deliver it. In the prevailing circumstances, however, and since the component agencies are already in place and operation, it is the nature of the functional relationships between them and the change required to these relationships that requires specification before a strategy can be determined.

Put another way, without a consensus for change being reached among those agencies that must be involved in its implementation, no strategy can stand a chance of successful delivery. In default of the necessary consensus, strategy specification becomes wasteful of effort and resources. The consensus therefore has to be based primarily upon the *necessity for change* rather than the nature of the change itself.

Justifiability Considerations

The earlier chapters of this work have clearly indicated a range of reasons why the prevailing criminal justice ideology based upon a retributive model of desert has become unjustifiable, given that at least one alternative model is available for consideration. The primary reasons may be summarised as follows:

- It does not deliver to the principal stakeholders in criminal justice the nature and quality of justice administration that each deserves.
- It has resulted in an unaffordable overuse of prison custody, and in particular of short-term sentencing, that is not conducive to reducing recidivism.
- Excessive use of prison custody creates overcrowding conditions that prevent prisons from delivering safe and purposeful regimes which address the causes of criminal behaviour and recidivism.
- A dominant emphasis on retrospective punitive retribution and incapacitation in sentencing precludes an appropriate focus on those most harmed by crime – victims and communities.
- Victims of crime have a positive desert claim to consideration and compensation (or reparation) because the harm caused to them is not self-inflicted, and this legitimate

desert claim is largely unacknowledged by the retributive desert model of criminal punishment.

- Those who cause this harm (offenders) deserve an opportunity to acknowledge their wrongdoing, take responsibility for it, and make reparation to victims as a means of restoration to full citizenship. Neither present prison conditions nor community sanctions facilitate this desert claim adequately.
- Imprisonment should be reserved for use only where it is strictly unavoidable, and for the shortest duration appropriate to the gravity of offences. Courts should be required to state, when sentencing, precisely why no other non-custodial alternative sanction would suffice in the circumstances, and how the term imposed is deserved by, and proportionate to, the seriousness of the offence(s).
- Imprisonment imposed for public protection should only be permitted where it can be shown that the offender poses a obvious and continuing risk to public safety that prison custody is capable of reducing rather than merely containing.

If and when a consensus for change can be achieved that each of these considerations is reasonable and necessary, then a strategy to deliver the desired outcomes can and should be devised. Such a strategy must be capable of accommodating and adequately meeting each of the desert claims indicated above.

In Chapter 8, it will be assumed that such a consensus can be built between the various stakeholders within the criminal justice process (the state, judiciary, criminal justice professionals and administrators etc.) and those other agencies and interest groups (politicians, academics, victim support groups, the media, penal reformers and the public) with a legitimate interest in the specification and delivery of the strategy for change.

Here, however, brief mention should be made of the work of the former Advisory Council on the Penal System (ACPS), which was set up in 1966 to advise the government on penal policy and operational issues.[15] If a similar body were in existence now, or in a modified form, it might prove to be invaluable as a means of consensus building with a membership drawn from the key strategic institutions mentioned earlier in this chapter.

On a note of caution, however, it is the purpose of this work to indicate how, and to what extent, a reshaping of the concept of desert explains why such change is necessary. It is beyond its scope to specify how this change should be implemented in detail. Instead

15 The ACPS was formed on the initiative of the then Home Secretary, Roy Jenkins, under the initial chairmanship of Kenneth (later Sir) Younger. Between 1968 and 1978 it published a number of influential reports on the reform of the penal system which were incorporated into legislation or operational practice. The council drew its membership from a wide range of persons with particular expertise on penal matters, having standing members and other participants drawn from academic institutions, the judiciary, professional bodies and government departments. Its work was discontinued in 1978/9 when the government headed by Margaret Thatcher and her Home Secretary, William Whitelaw, came into office, and was never replicated subsequently in a formal sense.

it is intended to identify the principles and strategy upon which the necessary change should be based in the interests of 'doing justice better'. If this much is achieved, the work will have realised its purpose.

8 Evolving a Strategy

Strategy Deliberation

From the previous chapter, it may be affirmed that a consensus to build and deliver a fairer and more effective criminal justice system in England and Wales requires a clear and unequivocal strategic aim. This aim must be to reduce the number of persons sentenced to imprisonment to a level that is affordable in fiscal terms, while also meeting the legitimate desert claims of all the stakeholders in criminal justice.

Reducing the use of imprisonment implies a corresponding increase in the use of non-custodial sanctions that would require capital investment. However, if the rate of imprisonment *per* hundred thousand of the population of England and Wales were to be reduced from the present level of 148 to one more consistent with the neighbouring countries of Western Europe (Scotland 146; the Netherlands 82; Portugal 138; Austria 98; Germany 78; Belgium 108; France 103, Switzerland 87; Sweden 60; Northern Ireland 101; Finland 58; Norway 72 – Mean = 94.25), then the average daily prison population would have to drop to around 51,000 from the March 2015 figure of 85,000 (International Centre for Prison Studies, 2014 ; BBC, 2014: 1; Howard League for Penal reform, 2015: 1). In 1994, the average daily prison population of England and Wales was 48,621 (Prison Reform Trust, 2014: 4). Table 8.1 indicates the progressive average daily prison population reduction rates *per* hundred thousand based upon an England and Wales population of 56 Million inhabitants.

Table 8.1 Average Daily Prison Population: 100,000 of Population[1]

Average daily prison population reductions to match imprisonment rates *per* 100,000 of population in England and Wales

	Rate *per* 100,000 E&W Population	Average Daily Prison Population	Cumulative Reduction
	145	81,200	
CNA Level →	140	78,400	2,800 = 3.44%
	135	75,600	5,600 = 6.89%
	130	72,800	8,400 = 10.34%
	125	70,000	11,200 = 13.79%
	120	67,200	14,000 = 17.24%
	115	64,400	16,800 = 20.68%
	110	61,600	19,600 = 24.13%
	105	58,800	22,400 = 27.58%
	100	56,000	25,200 = 31.03%
	95	53,200	28,000 = 34.48%
	90	50,400	30,800 = 36.94%

The present un-crowded (CNA or certified normal accommodation) level of occupancy of all prisons in England and Wales is 77,358 as at 14 September 2015, and this is the Prison Service's own measure of how many prisoners can be held in decent and safe accommodation with planned regimes delivered (Howard League for Penal reform, 2015: 1, but see Note 11 below). At the present rate of occupancy (85,083) some 8,325 prisoners (11%) are held above this level. Both the present prison population level and the rate *per* hundred thousand of population are the highest in Western Europe, and the percentage occupancy rate of 112.7% is the third highest after Italy (131.5%) and Spain (129.5) (Id.).[2]

In the year ending March 2014, the number of offenders sentenced to immediate custody in England and Wales was 91,895: a slight reduction on the previous year. Of these, 48,122 were sentenced at the crown court and 43,773 by magistrates' courts. Also, of the total number thus sentenced, 57% (52,380) were imprisoned for six months or less, and 37.6% (34,606) for periods up to and including three months (Prison Reform Trust, 2014: 22). Given that all of these offenders would spend only a maximum of three months in custody and be released unconditionally (without supervision) on the expiry of their sentences, and the extent of overcrowding in prisons mentioned earlier, it is altogether unlikely that anyone, apart from a very small proportion of these people, would receive any assistance

1 Data extracted from ICPS (2014).

2 The latter two countries were excluded from the list of those Western European countries quoted earlier due to their excessive occupancy rates of existing prison accommodation.

towards avoiding reconviction in the future. As a recent report by HM Inspectorate of Prisons indicated with reference to the impact of overcrowding:

> Overcrowding is not simply an issue of how many prisoners can be crammed into the available cells, but also affects whether the staff and other resources are available to keep them purposefully occupied and reduce the likelihood [that] they will reoffend. A prisoner who is unemployed because there is no activity available for him might spend up to 22 hours a day and eat all his meals, with another prisoner in a small cell designed for one, perhaps eight foot by six foot, with an unscreened toilet (HMCIP, 2013; quoted in Prison Reform Trust. 2014: 19).

This is the almost neglectful contemporary scenario against which the strategy for reduction has to be devised but, as will be seen subsequently, it opens up a range of options for reduction and reform of imprisonment in England and Wales as in other countries where such conditions exist. It is a direct legacy of the punitive desert model that has dominated penal policy making and legislation for the past two decades, and which will continue to do so unless, or until, that model is replaced by another which is considerably more constructive and reasonable.

Defining the Strategic Aims and Assumptions

Every model or paradigm for strategic change requires a set of philosophical and operational assumptions upon which the change process must be based and promoted. In this instance the preferred replacement model is the reparative desert paradigm, which provides both the philosophical underpinning and the operational basis upon which options for change may be considered. Though this model does not entirely exclude a retributive element for the most serious offences in its bifurcated approach to sentencing, its emphasis is upon reducing the extent of avoidable imprisonment and upon meeting the legitimate desert claims of victims, offenders and communities.

A cardinal principle of strategic change management is that its aims and planning assumptions must be unequivocal and non-conflicting. Therefore, in the present instance the aims may be stated as:

1. To reduce and restrict the average daily prison population to a maximum level that is operationally viable without overcrowding (CNA – 5%),[3] and to a reduced overall level if possible.
2. To remove the option of immediate short-term custodial sentencing[4] from the penalty structure by replacement with demanding community sanctions combined with suspended custodial sentence provisions.
3. To maximise the provision for, and use of, reparative sentencing measures in both the custodial and community settings for those offenders assessed as suitable for such regimes.
4. To reserve the traditional mode of imprisonment for serious offenders who represent a significant public risk; or who are sentenced to more than twenty-four effective months in custody;[5] or who are deemed behaviourally unsuitable for participation in reparative regimes.[6]

Given these aims of a reformed penal system, it is appropriate to list the fundamental assumptions that would underpin the delivery of them. In the instance of England and Wales, these assumptions might be summarised as follows:

Assumption A

That a forum of interested parties can be formed, and that these parties would actively participate in a consultative process to promote a consensus over the reforms necessary to meet the aims stated. Further, that the participants would include, at the least, the law enforcement agencies indicated in Figure 7.2 augmented by representation from the Parole Board, academic institutions, penal reform groups,[7] victim support agencies, and the media.

3 To the level of total certified normal accommodation (CNA) less a percentage allowance for accommodation under repair or refurbishment, or a lesser overall population level if this is achievable in terms of sentencing and public risk.

4 Initially, sentences to effective imprisonment for six months or less in favour of community-based sanctions of a supervised and reparative nature with evident penal content.

5 Such would be offenders sentenced to four years imprisonment or longer whose effective sentence lengths in custody under present release conditions would be twenty-four months or longer unless released under existing parole arrangements.

6 These would be those offenders who are impenitent or unwilling to make reparation to victims of crime, or whose behavioural characteristics would disrupt reparative regimes.

7 Such as, for instance, the Howard League for Penal Reform, the Prison Reform Trust, the International Centre for Prison Studies (ICPS), and Prison Reform International.

Assumption B

That in the event that a significant majority consensus for reform were to be reached, the ministers of state within the key strategic institutions (see Figure 7.1), including the judiciary, would combine to present the proposals for reform to parliament in legislative form.

Assumption C

That financial savings resulting from a reduction in the use of imprisonment and a decrease in the custodial penal population would be directly transferred to meet the additional cost of expanded community correctional services for the delivery of the reform package.

Assumption D

That adoption of the reforms, if implemented, would involve the creation of a professional mediation service to work in conjunction with the police and prosecution services where, in a pre-trial setting, liaison between offenders and victims would take place, were it deemed appropriate, for negotiating reparation, apology and remorse to be conveyed to the courts.

Assumption E

That in the event that the reforms were implemented, there would need to be a considerably more complementary relationship between the existing prison and probation services, ideally perhaps in a unified correctional services structure within the Ministry of Justice.

Assumption F

That in Britain, as in most Western European countries, the levels of reported and recorded crime have decreased and stabilised over the past two decades, and it seems likely that this trend will continue. However, the United Kingdom remains a relatively 'high crime society' when measured against the 35 countries surveyed in the OECD comparative study updated to 2012 (Civitas, 2012 *passim*).[8] Crimes of violence short of intentional homicide largely account for this situation, being evident in the offences of robbery, assault and, to a lesser extent, rape.

---

8 Here, see; www.civitas.org.uk/crime/comments.php. There are, however, some problems of comparability within the OECD statistics due to variations in the methods of counting adopted by participating countries. These statistics are referenced as: Civitas, 2012.

Consideration of the aims and assumptions identified above leads logically to identification of the options for strategic reform of the criminal justice process in the present situation. It will be evident that these options are contingent upon the necessary consensus being created, and the timeframe within which implementation of the reforms might be envisaged. Moreover, since the desirable reform measures are of both an ideological and a structural nature, resort to further quick-fix solutions is ruled out in the particular circumstances.

Some reservation has been expressed earlier concerning the extent to which what is widely described as the 'criminal justice system' is, in reality, a system. Both Sir Louis Blom-Cooper (2013: 151-170) and earlier Andrew Rutherford (1986: 22) have expressed considerable doubt about this situation, the latter in the following extract from his work *Prisons and the Process of Justice* with which I entirely concur:

> It is important to place stress on the word *process* as there is a frequent and misleading tendency to view criminal justice as a system. Criminal justice as a system suggests an articulation of purposes and a degree of coordination and coherence which bears no resemblance to reality. One consequence of the systems approach is to invite expectations of criminal justice which cannot be achieved. Alternatively, to view criminal justice as a process allows an appreciation of the loose interconnections between the various stages, of sometimes competing goals between and within agencies, of the dynamic nature of the forces which determine shape and direction, of the informal nature of much of what takes place, and of the unanticipated consequences which not infrequently ensue. (Rutherford, 1986: 22)

The figures included in the preceding chapter and that which follows provide some compelling evidence of this situation, particularly in the relationships between the prison and probation services within NOMS and the Ministry of Justice, and between that Ministry, the Home Office and the Judiciary. This is a difficult issue to resolve since it places a focus upon the monolithic nature of several departments of state each of which have become accustomed to exercising a considerable extent of autonomy, and some of which have other functional responsibilities beyond that of criminal justice delivery.

Assessing the Strategic Options

Table 8.2 provides a summary of the prison population of England and Wales at the end of June 2014 by sentence length.

Table 8.2 Prison Population of England and Wales by Sentence Length at 30 June 2014

Sentence Length	Total
Up to or equal to 6 months	4,569
Over 6 months to less than 12 months	2,081
12 months	1,271
Over 12 to 18 months	2,980
Over 18 months to 3 years	11,210
Over 3 years up to 4 years	3,854
4 years	2,689
Over 4 to 5 years	4,839
Over 5 to 10 years	13,298
Over 10 years	5,534
Mandatory Life	5,228
*Imprisonment for Public Protection (IPP)	5,118
+Other Life Sentences	2,241
Recalls to Prison	5,620
Total Sentenced Prisoners	**71,361**
Remand Prisoners	12,197
Total in Prison Custody	**83,558**

Notes:
* Residue of IPP sentenced prisoners remaining after sentence abolished
+ Includes Discretionary Life and Automatic Life Sentenced Prisoners
Source: www.gov.uk/government/uploads/system/attachments_data/file/339036/prison-population-2014.xls (Accessed 10 February 2015), (Ministry of Justice 2014h).

In assessing the options available for reducing this population without a significant increase in public risk, it is logical to select two particular groups of these prisoners for closer examination: those held on remand un-sentenced (12,197); and those serving terms of twelve months or less (7,921) which together account for 20,118 (or 24.08%) of the total held in custody. In the case of the former group, in the twelve months ending in March 2014, 11% were subsequently acquitted and 16% went on to receive a non-custodial sentence at trial. Similar proportions would suggest that almost 3,300 of those held on remand on 30 June 2014 might attract similar disposals (Ministry of Justice, 2014c, Table 1.1). In the latter case, the maximum effective custodial period that would fall to be served by such prisoners would be six months or in many instances less, on expiry of which they would, in any event, be released unconditionally under current statutory provisions.[9]

9 Under the terms laid down in the Criminal Justice Act 1991.

Assuming once again that a consensus can be reached over the necessity for significant penal reform, and that therefore no quick fixes are contemplated, it will become necessary to determine the options available for achieving a reduction in the prison population to a desired and defined level, and the timeframe in which this is to be implemented. Table 8.1 may assist us in this process, bearing in mind that the present un-crowded occupancy level of the prisons estate in England and Wales stands at 76,758.

The options may be defined as follows:

Option 1

To select a rate of imprisonment *per* hundred thousand of the population that is more consistent with the rates to be found in other Western European countries with similar democratic traditions and economic circumstances. If, for example, a rate of 130 were to be considered appropriate, this would lower the prison population to around 70,000 with a corresponding reduction requirement of some 8,200 places. If, alternatively, the rate in Germany were to be selected, then the corresponding rates would need to be 95 *per* hundred thousand, the population reduced to *circa* 53,000, and a reduction of 28,000 places envisaged.

Option 2

To decide upon the maximum un-crowded accommodation level[10] of prison places that is affordable in fiscal terms and which will form the upper limit of occupation that will not be exceeded – a revised statement of CNA. Thus, for example, if a maximum capacity figure of 70,000 places were selected, a reduction of the present population of around 11,200 would be required, and the rate *per* hundred thousand of the population would fall to 125. In the event that the upper occupation limit became threatened however, it would be necessary to legislate procedures for releasing those prisoners closest to sentence expiry in order to accommodate new prisoners.

Option 3

To determine the extent of reduction that abandonment of short-term custodial sentencing (*i.e.* twelve months or less) would deliver in combination with a similar abandonment of overcrowding (reduction of places to existing CNA), and declare this to be the maximum

10 Less a 5% margin for accommodation taken out of use for repair or refurbishment purposes.

operational capacity of the prisons estate. Thus, from Table 8.2, the reduction in short-term prisoners would release some 7,900 places, the reduction to existing CNA would make 76,758 the available operational capacity, and this would comfortably exceed the required residual population capacity of *circa* 73,300 places, while at the same time lowering the rate *per* hundred thousand of population to around 131.

Option 4

To examine the feasibility of removing the remand population (12,587) from the prisons estate in its entirety, since all these prisoners are un-sentenced and should not morally be subjected to punitive prison regimes in advance of being sentenced. Since a significant proportion of those held in prisons on remand (*circa* 27%) are also subsequently acquitted at trial or are given non-custodial sentences, it would be preferable for them to be accommodated in another form of suitably secure accommodation supervised by a separate custodial entity under the *aegis* of HM Courts and Tribunals Service, and in locations close to the courts in which they will be brought up for trial and sentencing. If this were done in conjunction with abandonment of sentences of six months or less (4,569) and reduction of the prison population to CNA level, an overall reduction of over 17,000 prison places might be envisaged. In so doing, the occupation rate of prisons would fall to 64,200 (or 115 *per* hundred thousand of population) against a present CNA level of 76,758, and open up the opportunity to close entirely a number of existing older and cost-intensive prison establishments, and/or abandon plans to build further prisons.

These are some of the options for strategic reduction of the prison population, and further options might arise from other combinations of the measures considered. The justification for reduction remains, in each of these strategic options, both morally and operationally substantiated. It is, however, evident that the starting point for achieving any reductive strategy must be the process of deciding upon that level of penal population without overcrowding which is both sustainable and affordable in England and Wales in the short and longer terms.

The Place of Desert in Strategy Evolution

Removal of an individual's liberty and to a considerable extent also their personal autonomy, for however short or long a period of time, are very serious and possibly life-changing matters. Prisons are, at best, uncongenial and threatening places into which many inmates, newly convicted, arrive – at least for the first time – in a state of shock and genuine fear of what awaits them. Being locked into a confined space from which a prison officer walks away bearing the key can be a traumatic experience and, in the event that the space is already occupied by another inhabitant one has never set eyes upon, becomes a nightmarish situation. Such is just the start of the imprisonment process for many thousands of offenders each year within our post-modern democracies. They may respond to it with resignation, disbelief, defiance, aggression or even self-harming behaviour, all of which is atypical of their normal pattern of life beyond the custodial setting.

To an extent, and whatever offences they have committed, these people are casualties of our social environments. Some are inadequate, some are illiterate, some lack life and social skills, some are predatory, some are mentally disordered or addicted, some are manipulative or exploitive, some are sexually deviant, and a few are inherently wicked or incorrigible. The common denominator is that all are prisoners as an outcome of having committed criminal offences.

If our correctional purpose is to attempt to transform these people into adequately functional and law-abiding citizens, then what are their 'just deserts'? Visiting retributive punishment upon them for longer or shorter periods of time relative to the seriousness of their wrongdoing focuses entirely upon what they have been in the past, and has, at best, limited impact, however 'just' it may appear to be in relation to what cannot be undone. It is not part of the remit of correctional officials to pass judgement upon the nature or extent of offences: the courts have already undertaken that duty in convicting and sentencing offenders according to the provisions of the law. It is, however, part of the remit of correctional officials to deal with offenders impartially, in conditions of decency and safety, and encourage and assist them to become law-abiding and competent citizens in the future. That is what they deserve and have a right to expect of the correctional process.

Where overcrowded and inadequate conditions are perpetuated in prisons, the correctional purpose becomes subverted and incapable of delivery beyond that of incapacitation and containment. Moreover, it becomes altogether likely that exposure to such conditions and the hazards of life within them will result in offenders being returned into their societies embittered and unchanged by the prison experience. High rates of post-release recidivism reinforce the ineffectiveness of this excessively costly enterprise that displays such a marked extent of failure. Neither societies nor offenders deserve such outcomes.

To make matters even worse, this enterprise so 'unfit for purpose' continues to neglect and marginalise those most affected by its failure: victims of crime. This is the hallmark of the retributive desert model of criminal punishment that has recurred throughout this work with its emphasis on the past rather than the care and welfare of those most harmed by crime, and who also have positive desert claims to reparation that remain largely unaddressed.

Thus, whatever form of strategy is devised and adopted to remedy this situation must address these deficits in a deliberate and substantive manner. Offenders, victims and communities all deserve better and more effective justice, which might well be made deliverable by a determined policy of penal reform and a reduction in the social and fiscal costs of excessive imprisonment. In the chapter that follows we shall explore how a strategic model of reparative justice might fulfil this urgent social need.[11]

11 The reader may wish to note that at the time of final revision of this book prior to publication (September 2015) the total prison population of England and Wales had risen from the level of 83,558 indicated for June 2014 in Table 8.2 to that of 85,699, comprising 81,780 males and 3,919 females. The remand population stood at 11,785, a slight reduction from 12,197 recorded here. The distribution of these populations by sentence length and offence group remained broadly similar to the June 2014 figures. Source: The Howard League for Penal Reform Weekly Prison Watch, 2015, based on Ministry of Justice statistics, and available at: www.howardleague.org/weekly-prison-watch (Accessed 14 September 2015).

9 A Reparative Justice Model

Reparation: (1) the act or process of making amends (or compensation):
(2) the act or process of repairing or the state of having been repaired
[C14 *reparacioun* – ultimately from Latin *reparāre* to repair]
Collins English Dictionary (1983: 1236).

What is Reparative Justice?

Consideration of the definition provided above may assist the discussion that will follow in this chapter in which an explanation of the potential benefits of adopting a reparative approach to criminal justice will be offered. Such an approach cannot be applicable to all criminal offenders, but it may have a significant relevance for those presently sentenced to short terms of imprisonment as a community-based alternative to custody, and for others in custody serving longer terms but who are approaching their scheduled release dates.

Reparative justice is an integral element of restorative justice in a strictly operational sense that involves a considerable extent of voluntarism, without which it becomes relatively meaningless. This voluntarism extends to all the main stakeholders in the criminal justice process – offenders, victims of crime, communities and, ultimately, the state. It entails a willingness on the part of all of these stakeholders to enter into a process of mediation that is professionally overseen and supervised, the focus of which is to meet the legitimate desert claims of all the parties involved in, or affected by, criminal offending. It is, therefore, to a considerable extent, a form of communitarian justice.[1]

Here, it will be recalled from earlier chapters that within the context of this work the concept of 'corrections' is primarily one that involves changing offending behaviour into law-abiding behaviour. It relies to a greater extent upon persuasion rather than coercion; upon creation of awareness of the harm done to others; and upon willingness in offenders to make amends, and in those offended against to extend forgiveness where this is possible.

The process of making reparation logically precedes that of restoration, the latter being dependent upon, and consequent to the former. Reparation is, therefore, a means by which offenders may regain the status and benefits of full citizenship. Reparative justice is thus

1 By the term 'communitarian' is inferred here that form of justice prevalent in many areas of the world in which the emphasis in settling disputes relating to anti-communal behaviour lay within the cohesive nature of communities to resolve. It is still evident among first nation peoples of almost every continent worldwide as the preferred means of reaching just outcomes to the satisfaction of all the parties affected by such behaviour without resort to state-enforced intervention.

about the nature and extent of the restitutive action that offenders must undertake before being considered restored to full community status. In many respects it relates to the ancient doctrine of expiation common to many religions as a means of atoning for wrongdoing or 'sin'.

Figure 9.1 Reparative Justice Model

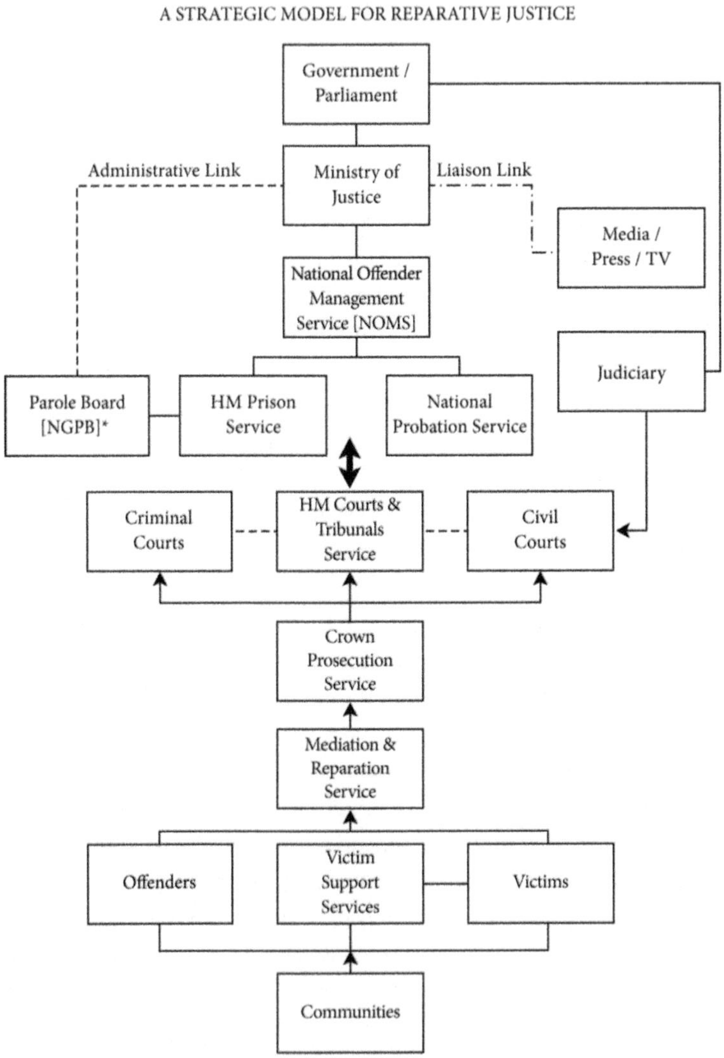

*Note: The Parole Board is a Non-Governmental Public Board [NGPB]

Such a concept is not without a number of attendant problems. It assumes, in the first place, that the offender is willing to show genuine remorse for the harm done to others, offer apology, and take responsibility for 'putting wrongs right'. This raises the issue of how the genuineness such remorse can be ascertained prior to its becoming acceptable as a basis for making reparation. In the second place, it raises the equally difficult issue of which forms of offences, and the relative seriousness of the harm done in commission of them, should qualify for consideration within reparative justice provisions and arrangements.[2] It is necessary to address these issues early in this discussion, and to this end I do so in the section that follows.

THE IMPORTANCE OF MEDIATION IN REPARATIVE JUSTICE

A strategic model for delivery of reparative justice is illustrated in Figure 9.1, and attention is drawn to the presence of a mediation and reparation service to which the various stakeholders should have access in cases in which a reparative outcome of offences is considered acceptable and desirable. It will also be noted that this service is linked directly to the prosecution authority, and thence to the courts.

Mediation between offenders and victims in the criminal justice process is a professional skill for which specific training and personal competencies are required to exacting and accredited levels of assurance. Much of the existing training in mediation techniques is oriented towards disputes resolution in the industrial, educational and other spheres of public life that are far removed from the criminal justice setting, even though some may be transferable or amenable to adaptation.

There are also recognisable risks in the specific area of criminal justice mediation between offenders and victims that include those of intimidation, manipulation, retraumatisation, insincerity and the like, and particularly in relation to the genuineness of remorse and its reliable assessment. These are matters for experienced professional judgement by mediators, without which reparative justice could easily come into disrepute.

In cases where mediated outcomes might be considered appropriate and satisfactory to all the parties involved in that process, it would be essential that a close professional relationship should be formed between mediation officials and those of the prosecution authority whose duty it would become to make a recommendation to this effect to the courts. Logically, this same level of relationships would be desirable between mediation

2 Here, I am grateful to my friend and colleague Professor John Blad of the School of Law, Erasmus University, Rotterdam, the Netherlands, for raising these important issues in correspondence over this work. I trust that he may be assured to some extent by the explanations that I provide subsequently, while recognising that these may retain an extent of indefinite expression that might not entirely satisfy the most particular of criminal lawyers.

and probation officials having responsibility to the courts for the casework supervision and assistance of offenders in the community, and to a lesser extent in custody.

There is now an extensive literature within the fields of psychiatry, psychology and to a lesser extent in criminology dealing with the issues of, *inter alia*, shame and remorse within the area of offender assessment in mediation and related contexts (*e.g.* Shapland *et al.*, 2006; Braithwaite, 2000; Brown, 2001; Tangney, Stuevig & Hafez, 2011), many with extensive bibliographical listings. Some of this literature is specifically oriented towards restorative justice interventions and their mediation.[3] Few of these works, however, include other than protocols for the assessment rather than the measurement of remorse, which would suggest that this presently remains more subjective than definitive in practice. Such is not to underrate the value of trained professional expertise and judgement in such matters, but rather to imply that, like sentencing decisions, there may always be a liability to subjective variability within the outcomes.

3 In particular the works of Shapland *et al.*, 2006, Braithwaite, 2000, and Tangney *et al.*, 2011, cited above.

Table 9.2 Prison Population under Immediate Custodial Sentences by Sentence Length, Offence Group and Sex (30 June 2014, England and Wales) – All Males up to and including 4 Years imprisonment

Ser	Sentence Length/Offence	Violent Offences	Sexual Offences	Robbery	Burglary	Theft / HSG*	Fraud / Forgery	Drug Offences	Motoring Offences	Other Offences	Not Recorded	TOTAL
1	6 months or less	919	79	30	144	1,310	70	110	270	1,045	85	4,062
2	Over 6 to 12 months	417	103	47	190	457	65	141	92	379	21	1,912
3	12 months	261	110	65	136	145	57	127	55	215	0	1,171
4	Over 12 to 18 months	778	249	138	441	272	100	305	115	399	0	2,797
5	Over 18 months to 3 yrs	1,722	869	1,066	2,458	745	311	2,313	143	989	2	10,618
6	Over 3 up to 4 yrs	466	279	574	805	206	103	973	20	284	0	3,710
7	4 years	407	331	455	398	99	88	568	8	208	0	2,562
8	Totals	4,970	2,020	2,375	4,572	3,234	794	4,537	703	3,519	108	26,832

* denotes Handling Stolen Goods

Table 9.3 Prison Population under Immediate Custodial Sentences by Sentence Length, Offence Group and Sex (30 June 2014, England and Wales) – All Females up to and including 4 Years Imprisonment

Ser	Sentence Length/Offence	Violent Offences	Sexual Offences	Robbery	Burglary	Theft / HSG*	Fraud / Forgery	Drug Offences	Motoring Offences	Other Offences	Not Recorded	TOTAL
1	6 months or less	68	4	1	10	273	20	16	9	99	7	507
2	Over 6 to 12 months	21	3	2	10	67	12	5	5	42	2	169
3	12 months	22	3	2	5	26	13	6	0	23	0	100
4	Over 12 to 18 months	41	4	15	21	38	13	17	2	32	0	183
5	Over 18 months to 3 yrs	91	12	65	74	76	58	108	8	100	0	592
6	Over 3 up to 4 yrs	24	1	22	16	10	13	38	0	20	0	144
7	4 years	24	2	23	9	9	7	29	0	24	0	127
8	Totals	291	29	130	145	499	136	219	24	340	9	1,822

Source: Prison Population by Sentence Length - 30 June 2014, London: Ministry of Justice, Table A1.17 available at, and extracted from: www.gov.uk/uploads/system/attachments_data/file/339036/prison-population-2014.xls. (Accessed 18 February 2015).

Offenders and Offences Amenable to Mediated Resolution

Reference to the Standard List of Offences in England and Wales reveals a very considerable array of acts defined as criminal in various forms of classification.[4] There is no specific means of separation of these offences into categories of seriousness, though the categories are codified in a generic sense such as between violent, sexual, acquisitive, fraudulent and other classes, and within these classes into actual, attempted and other forms. In a more general sense, it is the maximum penalty structure for each offence type that indicates its level of seriousness.

Examination of the sentencing structure in England and Wales, as amended since the legislation within the Criminal Justice Act 2003 became effective in April 2005 in respect of imprisonment for public protection and extended sentence for public protection (IPP and ESPP), reveals several changes in the punishment of the most serious criminal offences.[5] Though these changes need not detain the reader here, it must be suggested that certain categories of sentenced offenders must, by nature of their sentence lengths, be excluded from further consideration in this particular discussion.[6]

Tables 9.2 and 9.3 indicate the number of sentenced offenders in England and Wales on 30 June 2014 who were serving terms of imprisonment for four years or less by offence groups, sentence lengths and sex.[7] Under present circumstances, the effective custodial period[8] for all of these 28,654 male and female prisoners would be two years or less in duration, although in the cases of those 2,689 prisoners serving sentences of four years, they could be retained in prison rather than on discretionary conditional release (DCR)

---

4 See: www.gov.uk/government/uploads/.../offence-classifications.xls (Accessed 14 February 2015), or as an alternative: www/doc.ukdataservice.ac.uk/doc/3935/mrdoc/word/01codes.doc which displays the same information in a different format (Accessed 14 February 2015).

5 Insofar as the Criminal Justice and Immigration Act 2008 introduced a new 'seriousness threshold' for IPPs which were becoming considerably overused by the courts, and had resulted in serious delays in the Parole Board's reviews of 'tariff-expired' prisoners for release. This was achieved by amendment to the Criminal Justice Act 2003 legislation effective from 14 July 2008. IPPs were eventually abolished in the Legal Aid, Sentencing and Punishment of Offenders Act 2012 (Article 6) which introduced a new mandatory life sentence for serious violent and sexual offenders convicted of repeat offences listed within schedule 15B of CJA 2003, and new provisions for extended sentences (in s.125). For further explanation see, Strickland and Grimwood 2013.

6 These include those serving sentences of mandatory life imprisonment (or the equivalent for those aged under 21 years), discretionary life sentences, automatic life sentences, extended sentences (LASPO Act 2012, s.124), and other determinate sentences of an extent to be debated subsequently here.

7 The statistical data within this chapter are based upon June 2014 official tables as indicated. Corresponding data as at the time of final revision of this work (September 2015) await publication, which has prevented updating.

8 Such is to indicate that period of the total sentence to be spent in prison custody prior to release unconditionally, or subject to conditional or discretionary release arrangements under supervision by the National Probation Service.

from the 24 months to 32 months period of sentence before gaining automatic conditional release (ACR) at the 36 month point.

From the tables it will also be noted that a total of 7,921 (7,145 male and 776 female) prisoners were serving terms of twelve months or less with effective custodial periods of six months or less in the majority of cases. These were the cohorts of prisoners for whom it was suggested earlier that such sentences might be largely abandoned in favour non-custodial alternative provisions, since their offences would predominantly lie within the less serious range. If this reduction could be achieved, then the total number of prisoners serving sentences of four years or less would drop from 28,654 to 20,713 serving sentences of between twelve months and four years in duration.

Of this remainder, 15,505 (14,586 males and 919 females) were serving sentences of over 12 months and up to three years, with effective sentence periods of between six and eighteen months in duration. A further 3,854 (3,710 males and 144 females) would also remain to be considered, serving sentences of over three years up to four years imprisonment, and with effective sentence lengths of between eighteen and twenty-four months in custody. It is from these specific groups of offenders that suitable candidates for reparative prison regimes might be envisaged as being forthcoming, and with a potential (given appropriate skills training and structured regimes) for reducing post-release recidivism. Based upon the June 2014 prison population statistics, the residual prison population of 54,048 reduced by the measures outlined above would have the following profile:

Table 9.4 Residual Prison Population by Sentence Length

Sentence Type	Population
Medium Term Prisoners:	4,839
Over 4 and up to 5 years imprisonment	13,298
5 years up to 10 years imprisonment	**18,137**
Total:	
Long Term Prisoners:	5,534
Over 10 years imprisonment	5,228
Mandatory life sentences	2,241
Other life sentences	5,118
Residue of IPP/ESPP sentences	**18,094**
Total:	
Recalls to custody:	**5,620**
Remand Prisoners:	**12,197**
Totals	**54,048**

Source: Data extracted from Table 8.2.

By way of summarising the prison population situation in England and Wales as at the mid-point of 2014, it may be helpful for the reader to view the various components within it as shown in the following table:

Table 9.5 Total Prison Population at 30 June 2014 by Sentence Bands

Status/Sentence	Males	Females	Total
Up to and including 12 months	7,145	776	7,921
Over 12 months to 4 years	19,928	1,079	21,007
Over 4 years determinate	23,827	759	24,586
Indeterminate (Life + IPP/ESPP)	12,205	382	12,587
Recalls to custody	5,418	202	5,620
Total Sentenced Prisoners	**68,163**	**3,198**	**71,361**
Remand Prisoners	11,503	694	12,197
Total in Prison Custody	**79,666**	**3,892**	**83,558***

Source: Extracted from Ministry of Justice (2014a), Table A1.17 and Prison Reform Trust (2014: 25) in respect of remand prisoners.
From Table 9.5, it should be noted *per* the * annotation in the total column that a discrepancy of 333 arises between that shown in Table 8.2 and this table. This is accounted for insofar as the source document contains within its data prisoners whose precise sentence length is not recorded, but who have been included within broad sentence bands on an estimated basis rather than in detailed sentence length bands. These persons may comprise that group recalled to custody having breached the conditions of conditional release, with residual sentence periods of lesser length than those originally imposed.

In the section of this chapter that follows, attention will be focused upon the data shown in Tables 9.2 and 9.3 which provide a detailed breakdown of the offence groups into which males and females serving sentences of between over twelve months and four years were divided on 30 June 2014. These offenders, it will be recalled, were those suggested as potentially suitable for the reparative custody regimes prescribed within this work.

CONSIDERING OFFENCES AMENABLE TO REPARATIVE SANCTIONS

The population under discussion here concerns only those 21,007 prisoners (19,928 males and 1,079 females) serving sentences of more than twelve months and up to (and including) four years imprisonment. The breakdown of their main offence groups is shown below.[9]

9 The offence group shown for each prisoner is that of the most serious offence convicted. Some prisoners may have been convicted of further and lesser offences, or have had other offences taken into consideration at trial, but these are not recorded here.

Table 9.6 Offence Categories – Prisoners Serving Over 12 Months to 4 Years

Offence Category	Males	Females	Totals	Code+
Drug-related offences	4,179	192	4,371	A-S
Burglary	4,115	122	4,237	IP(V)
Violence against person	3,403	183	3,586	IP(V)
Robbery	2,248	128	2,376	IP(V)
Other offences	1,897	181	2,078	-
Sexual offences	1,740	20	1,760	IP(V)
Theft/HSG*	1,328	134	1,462	A-S(V)
Fraud or forgery	606	92	698	A-S(V)
Motoring offences	286	10	296	A-S
Offence not recorded	126	17	143	-
Totals	**19,928**	**1,079**	**21,007**	

Source: Extracted from Ministry of Justice (2014), Table A1.17
Note: * Denotes handling stolen goods (HSG)
+ Key: A-S = anti-social: IP = interpersonal; (V) = victim involvement

From the table it will be evident that the majority of the offences indicated (56.5%) were of an interpersonal nature involving identifiable victims or entities, and a further and sizeable percentage (32.3%) were of a predominantly anti-social nature in which drug-related offences dominated. However, in considering mediation, the number of sexual offences (8.3%) – although relatively small – could involve some predictable difficulties.

From a punitive desert viewpoint, as Tables 9.2 and 9.3 indicate, the number of offences warranting sentences of over eighteen months and up to (and including) four years represented 61.9% of the total. It should also be noted in particular that within that proportion, the offences of violence against the person and robbery accounted for 27.1% of the overall number, and that these were relatively serious crimes of an interpersonal nature with clearly identifiable victims.

It will also be recalled (from Chapter 8) that, in evolving the strategy for reform of the penal system, one of the four principal aims was defined as 'maximising the use of reparative sentencing measures in both the custodial and the community settings for those offenders deemed suitable for such regimes'. This in turn posited the requirement for a professional mediation service closely allied to the Crown Prosecution Service and the victim support services as indicated in Figure 9.1.

The dilemma that arises from the situation outlined above is that of balancing what might be perceived as the conflicting aims of 'reducing and restricting the average daily prison population' (Strategic Aim 1), and 'maximising the use of reparative sentencing' (Strategic Aim 3) while at the same time meeting the legitimate desert claims of victims, offenders and communities.[10] For if it may be accepted that offenders deserve punishment for the harm they cause, they also have a positive desert claim to assistance towards adopting law-abiding lifestyles and restoration to full citizenship. Victims also have positive desert claims to reparation for the harm suffered by them through offences, and communities have a similar claim to a reduction in the rates of re-offending and the social disruption that it causes.

There is, of course, an element of potential public risk inherent in a wider use of community penalties in place of short custodial sentences. However, this risk has to be balanced against that of the crime-enhancing nature of prison regimes overcrowded to the extent that short-term prisoners receive minimal (if any) assistance to address the causes of their offending, or to make reparation through skills training and purposeful work. The high rates of re-offending within twelve months following release discussed earlier in this work are compelling evidence that the latter risk is at least equivalent to, if not greater than, the former.

Mediation between victims and offenders where both are willing to enter into its process presents potential for reconciliation between all the parties to criminal offending and a reduction in recidivism as an outcome. It also offers offenders an opportunity to understand the harm that they cause, to offer and make reparation, and for victims the possibility of feeling vindicated. Conducting mediation is, however, a professional skill that has to be acquired and delivered to high standards of assurance and reliability in which all the parties involved and the courts can have confidence. Face-to-face mediation need not be an absolute requirement in situations in which victims might be fearful of intimidation, since the role of the mediator can be fulfilled on a third-party basis as an intermediary between offenders and victims at least initially or until both parties agree to meeting together.

Many of the offences identified in this study could be resolved beneficially through mediation and reparation, even if reparation has to be made in a custodial setting initially due to the seriousness of the wrongdoing. Reparative custodial sentences for more serious offences should, however, include an integral transitional community-based element prior to release to test the ability of the offender to refrain from further crime for a specified period of time. In the final chapter of this book, we shall examine how this transitional process might work in operational practice.

10 In this connection, the desert claim of communities would be met by a reduction in recidivist crime by offenders taking part in reparative regimes in prisons, and while completing reparative projects within communities as part of enhanced non-custodial sanctions.

Making Reparation a Reality

If the concept of reparative justice is to become an integral element of the criminal justice process it would be essential to define the means by which reparation made by offenders would become compensation for victims of crime. Here it will be noted that in Figure 9.1 provision was made for a mediation and reparation service (M&RS) linked via the Crown Prosecution Service to the courts, and thence to the prison and probation services responsible for the administration and supervision of sentenced offenders in custody and in the community respectively. The reasoning for this proposal is closely linked to the concept of reparative prisons and community service which, within this strategy, would become the principal operational components of reparative justice delivery.

In cases in which persons charged with offences, either criminal or civil by definition, were prepared to accept and take responsibility for their guilt and make reparation, it would fall to the prosecution and mediation authorities in consultation to determine whether a mediated settlement should be recommended to the court at a preliminary hearing of the case. Where such a recommendation was approved, the case would be adjourned to permit mediation to take place, with a date set for a subsequent hearing. The preliminary hearing could appropriately be heard before a public prosecutor or an examining magistrate, as is the custom in a number of Western European countries.

Assuming a successful mediation outcome, the case could be brought to trial on a guilty plea, and it would fall to the court to make an order for reparation in conjunction with any further penalty it considered necessary in relation to the seriousness of the charge and the culpability of the offender. Thus in serious cases a sentence to reparative custody or a community penalty could be made in combination with an order for reparation. However, where an order for reparation alone became the outcome of the sentencing process, it would be appropriate for the court to specify a suspended sentence period of reparative custody that could be activated in default of the reparation being made completely.[11]

There is a danger at this stage of the discussion that the proposals made here may become over-prescriptive and the strategy too detailed. I have sought in this work to avoid such criticism since it is the task of penal policymakers to determine how the strategy can best be met in operational terms. There remain, notwithstanding, three issues of broad policy that would need to be addressed: the first of these is how the proceeds of reparation would be reliably accounted for; the second is how the reparation proceeds would be made available as compensation to victims of crime; and the third concerns how the required number of reparative prisons with un-crowded regimes and the necessary training and

11 On the basis that, if the suspended sentence were to be activated, the offender would be placed in a reparative prison where purposeful work with realistic wages would be available to enable the offender to make the required reparation prior to being discharged at sentence expiry or earlier if appropriate.

employment conditions could be provided and geographically dispersed throughout England and Wales.

As to the first issue, it would seem logical to suggest that the M&RS should be tasked with accounting for funds derived from reparation in conjunction with the National Offender Management Service (NOMS),[12] and thus that the M&RS should become an agency of the Ministry of Justice. In the second instance, sentencing officials (judges and magistrates) might be empowered when making reparation orders to specify whether the victim(s) in a particular case should receive compensation directly, or alternatively, where no victim is immediately identifiable,[13] the reparation funds should accrue to a central fund administered by the M&RS for the compensation of crime victims or communities in general upon application.

Finally, the issue of reparative prisons would have to be addressed, and in the present circumstances with some difficulty as we shall discover in Chapter 10 that follows. For based upon mid-2014 statistical data the following factors have to be considered:

1. The average daily prison population stood at 83,558.[14]
2. The average daily level of overcrowding was 19,383 (23%).[15]
3. Some 80 of the 118 existing prisons were overcrowded.
4. The un-crowded capacity of prisons was approximately 64,175.[16]
5. The remand population accounted for an average of 12,197 places daily.[17]

---

12 And thus through NOMS to the prison and probation services responsible for the supervision and administration of offenders sentenced to reparative custody or community penalties with reparation order requirements.

13 Here might be considered organisations or entities including communities which have suffered financial loss as a direct result of offences such as fraud, deception, theft (including shoplifting), criminal damage and similar crimes in the form of compensation.

14 It has since risen to 85,699 in September 2015.

15 Due to recent building and extension programme provision this has dropped – but see Note 17 below.

16 It has since increased to 77,358, leaving the average daily population some 8,161 over the measure of uncrowded capacity (11.8%). However, the reader will note that these statistics need to be treated with extreme caution since there remains a considerable difference between that measure originally identified as the certified normal accommodation (CNA) or baseline CNA uncrowded level of occupancy, and what has come to be known as the 'crowded or overcrowded capacity'. The former was that level of accommodation for which the prison was originally designed to provide, and the latter is that increased level of occupancy with cell sharing (i.e. two inmates sharing a cell originally designed for one, etc.) deemed to meet contemporary accommodation requirements with acceptable standards of safety and decency. These definitions are set out in Prison Service Order 1900 – Certified Prisoner Accommodation – Issue no. 133, London, HM Prison Service, 2001, in Annex B. The operational capacity of a prison is the total number of prisoners that an establishment can hold 'without a serious risk to good order, security and the proper running of the planned regime', determined by area managers using operational judgement. It is normally set to be equal to or greater than CNA or baseline CNA to allow for a safe level of overcrowding, but cannot exceed the sum of the certified maximum capacities of all the accommodation in use (hence, the term 'in-use CNA' which is baseline CNA less cells not available for immediate use due to damage, building works, refurbishment, or taken out of use due to staff shortages).

17 This figure has also fell during 2015 to around 11,785 at the time of final revision of this work.

6. The sentenced prison population included 5,260 offenders recalled to custody.
7. Abandonment of sentences of 12 months or less would release 7,921 places.
8. The potential reparative custody population serving sentences over 12 months and up to 4 years would require a maximum of 21,000 prison places.
9. The residual medium-term (over 4 years to 10 years) population stands at some 18,137 prison places.
10. The long-term (over 10 years and indeterminate sentence) population requires a further 18,121 places.[18]
11. Between 2011 and 2015 eighteen prisons were closed and the number of full-time equivalent staff reduced by 12,530.
12. For the 2014-15 financial year, NOMS is committed to a further savings target of £ 149 million, half of which has to be found by public sector prisons through its benchmarking and efficiency programme. (All Prison Reform Trust, 2014 *passim.*)

All of which means that any penal reform and restructuring agenda has to be considered against a situation in which the plan is to reduce overall operating costs, and the prison population is presently projected to rise or at best remain static.

18 This population includes mandatory life sentences, discretionary and automatic life sentences, and the remainder of the former imprisonment for public protection (IPP and ESPP) sentences still in force although the sentence has been abandoned.

10 Putting the Pieces Together

Preliminary Observations

The purpose of this book has been to focus attention upon what criminal and other offenders, their victims, and the communities in which they live deserve from the processes of justice. For more than four decades, it has been the fashion within the conversations relating to crime and penology to regard the concept of desert as the primary justification for retributive punishment alone. This work has challenged such a notion to a very considerable extent.

It has also been fashionable to regard the custodial penal population as an amorphous mass, segregated from day-to-day participation in normal community life for as long as the courts decide is justifiable in response to the relative seriousness of offences. Long past are the days when serious questions were asked about whether such segregation effectively reduced the likelihood of re-offending, or whether the size of the mass had any acceptable limits, or whether such a process was strictly necessary in the first place. It sufficed to presume that segregation was what the mass deserved, and that it was appropriate that this should be so.

The self-consciousness of the political discourses on crime and the need for social protection from it projected by the media within increasingly affluent democracies has fuelled the demand for increasing use of segregation and incapacitation to the extent that the mass had no finite limits. On repeated occasions in England and Wales, the size of the prison population exceeded the capacity of the penal estate to the point of crisis in the conditions in which those segregated were held, and the political response has been to increase the capacity rather than question the size of the mass. Worse still, perhaps, it seemed that questions about whether the conditions in which prisoners were confined achieved any desirable social purpose became largely irrelevant.[1]

And so by mid-2011, in an era of severe fiscal retrenchment in England and Wales, means had to be found of reducing the costs of containing the mass rather than reducing its size which had reached an all-time high of over 85,000. Between then and mid-2014 eighteen relatively small and cost-intensive prisons , many of them of out-dated design, were earmarked for closure. Plans were laid to design, build and open three new and larger

1 In 2013-14, an average of 19,383 prisoners (23% of the prison population) were held in overcrowded accommodation. The number doubling up in cells designed for single occupancy was 18,515 (22%) (House of Commons, 201412).

prisons to replace those closed, and also to extend the capacity of four existing prisons.[2] In addition, significant reductions in full-time equivalent prison staff (12,530 posts) were also planned and implemented between March 2010 and June 2014.

It is a matter of further concern that prisons in England and Wales are becoming more violent in the conditions indicated here. In 2013-14 there was a 35.3% increase in serious prisoner-on-prisoner assaults (from 1,227 to 1,661, including three homicides), and a 14.9% increase in prisoner assaults on staff (from 2,787 to 3,201). 2013-14 also saw the highest rate of suicides (88) since the previous highest year total of 2004-05 (87) (Travis, 2014).[3] It should also be noted that the ratio of prison officers to prisoners in 2000 was 1:2.9, but by late 2013 it had increased to 1:4.8 prisoners (House of Commons, 2007).

This is only part of the backdrop against which this study was conceived. For in spite of a raft of expansive statements by successive governments since 1990 purporting to give victims of crime due consideration, little of substance has emerged to make this a reality. Restorative justice has consistently promoted the basis upon which this might be achieved, but has been consigned to the margins of the criminal justice process because it poses questions about crime and punishment that are, and remain, beyond the boundaries of the contemporary political discourses.[4]

Thus in relation to the notion of desert within criminal justice, it became essential to look beyond the traditional retributive agenda to discover the various constituencies that might have legitimate desert claims on the justice process. These constituencies, as we have seen, consist chiefly in offenders, victims of crime, and the communities within which crime is committed. In addition, the dependents of both offenders and crime victims deserve due consideration. We therefore consider the desert claims of each of these constituencies in turn.

Offender Desert Claims in Custody

In considering the occupation of the prisons at mid-2014 levels, it is necessary to separate out the various sentence bands within their populations. For although it may be held that all those offenders sentenced to imprisonment have incurred that penalty due to the seriousness of their offences, the purpose of prisons should be to promote behavioural change

---

2 These new prisons comprise HMPs Thameside (capacity 900), Oakwood (1,605) opened in mid-2012, and a 2,100 place prison at Wrexham, North Wales, scheduled to open by late 2017. Building to expand existing capacity at HMPs Thameside, The Mount, Parc and Peterborough is currently underway (Prison Reform Trust, 2014: 18).

3 See: www.theguardian.com/society/2014/jul/31/official-figures-violence-prisons-england-wales (Accessed 3 March 2015).

4 Here, *e.g.* see, Home Office, 1990; Home Office, 1996; Home Office, 2003a and b: Home Office, 2005a, b, c and d; Ministry of Justice, 2012d, e and f.

before releasing back into communities ex-offenders so that they are less likely to re-offend in the future. Table 10.1 summarises the constituent elements of the mid-2014 prison population.

Table 10.1 Prison Population (England & Wales) at 30 June 2014 by Sentence Length*

Sentence Band/Status	Males	Females	Totals
Up to and including 12 months	7,145	776	7,921
Over 12 months to 4 years	19,928	1,079	21,007
Over 4 years determinate	23,700	886	24,586
Indeterminate sentenced	12,205	382	12,587
Recalls to custody	5,058	202	5,260
Total Sentenced Prisoners	**68,036**	**3,325**	**71,361**
Total Remand Prisoners	11,503	694	12,197
Totals in Prison Custody	**79,539**	**4,019**	**83,558**

Sources: Ministry of Justice, 2014, Table A1.17 and Prison Reform Trust, 2014: 25.
* The table shows a variance with the MoJ source document in that in 1,318 cases the precise sentence length was not recorded, but allocated on an estimated basis within broad sentence bands. The error has been corrected here.

From earlier discussion it will be recalled (in Chapter 8) that Strategic Aim 2 was to remove the option of short-term custodial sentencing (twelve months and less) from the penalty structure by replacement it with community sanctions. If this measure were to be implemented, it would reduce the total in prison custody from 83,558 (79,666 males and 3,892 females) to 75,637 (72,521 males and 3,116 females). The reasoning for this recommendation was that on the basis of statistical evidence on reconviction rates,[5] short prison sentences served in overcrowded conditions failed significantly to reduce re-offending, whereas community sentences had a considerably greater potential to do so. Many prisoners serving such sentences are held in local prisons which are among the most heavily overcrowded in the prison system.

Strategic Aim 1 was to reduce and restrict the overall prison population to the 'in-use' CNA level (less 5% for repair or refurbishment) as the measure of maximum capacity. In mid-2014 this un-crowded level stood at 75,695, and the reduction available from abandonment of short-term sentences would make this largely achievable without significant additional public risk.

Strategic Aim 3 was to maximise the provision for, and use of, reparative sentencing measures in both the custodial and community settings for those offenders assessed as suitable for such regimes. Those prisoners serving sentences of over twelve months and

5 Here, see, *e.g.* Ministry of Justice, 2014f, and Ministry of Justice, 2013d.

up to and including four years have effective sentence lengths of two years or less – a total of 21,007 (19,928 males and 1,079 females).[6] It is from this sentence band of offenders that those suitable for reparative prison regimes might appropriately be selected.[7] We shall return to this particular population in later discussion.

Strategic Aim 4 was to reserve the traditional mode of imprisonment for those serious offenders representing a significant public risk, or whose effective custodial periods were of over two years or more (over four years imprisonment), or who are deemed unsuitable for reparative custody regimes. Such prisoners would be those sentenced to over four years imprisonment, indeterminate sentences, or recall to custody having breached the conditions of their release or community sentences. This population amounted to 42,433 (40,963 males and 1,470 females), many of whom are presently held in doubled-up accommodation designed for single occupancy. Though they may be serious offenders serving long sentences, they deserve better and more decent conditions than are provided at present.

The final point of discussion in relation to the population in prison custody concerns remand prisoners – in mid-2014 numbering 12,197 (11,503 males and 694 females) – the males being held in local prisons which have the highest overcrowding rates of all in England and Wales. These prisoners are those awaiting trial, un-convicted or convicted but un-sentenced. There are many reasons why these people are lodged in prison custody before being sentenced by the courts, but a considerable proportion of them (estimated to be as many as 27% by the Prison Reform Trust, 2014: 4) are subsequently acquitted at trial or, if found guilty, attract a non-custodial sentence. Within the statistics shown here, the latter number might be as high as 3,293 (3,106 males and 187 females). As un-sentenced persons, it becomes questionable whether they should be subjected to the considerably overcrowded conditions of male prisons in particular, or rather whether some other more appropriate yet secure accommodation should be provided if this were possible, in conditions more suitable to their status and needs, and adjacent to the courts in which they must appear for trial.

One long-term solution to this problem might be to establish a separate custodial service with small secure units close to the Crown Courts in particular, and under the *aegis* of the Courts and Tribunals Service rather than the Prison Service. Under present circumstances, however, remand prisoners simply do not deserve the conditions and restrictions under which they are held, and their removal from the prisons estate would significantly improve the prevailing conditions in local prisons. In terms of numbers it would reduce the prison

6 However, those serving four years imprisonment have a liability to serve the period between the mid-point of sentence (2 years) and the two-thirds point (2 years and 8 months) in custody or on discretionary conditional release depending on their assessed progress and suitability for release. Those serving twelve months or more but less than four years attract automatic conditional release at the mid-point of their sentence.

7 Once a network of reparative prisons had become established and operational, it might also be appropriate to extend their use to longer-term prisoners in the final two years of their terms of prison custody and subject to careful assessment as to suitability.

population by 12,197 places (11,503 males and 694 females), and in combination with abandonment of short-term sentences (7,921 places), to a level of 63,440 (61,018 males and 2,422 females).

In summary, it is clearly evident that, due to the pressure of numbers, prisons are prevented from holding those in their charge under acceptable conditions and in regimes capable of encouraging behavioural change and reducing re-offending. Whatever the duration of sentences, prisoners have a desert claim to decent conditions and assistance towards adopting law-abiding lifestyles on release from custody. The majority of prisoners must eventually return to their communities, and these communities are placed at unnecessary risk of victimisation if the majority of those imprisoned re-offend within short periods of time following release from custody.

OFFENDER DESERT CLAIMS IN THE COMMUNITY CORRECTIONS SECTOR

Like offenders in custody, those sentenced to community penalties should expect that their wrongdoing will have consequences that make demands on them to take responsibility for their actions and make good, insofar as is possible, the harm they have imposed upon victims and communities. In order to repair this harm they must subject themselves to a disciplined and supervised lifestyle by addressing their offending behaviour and making reparation through purposeful work or activities for both victims and their communities. They must also understand and accept that failure to do so will result in the more severe sanction of imprisonment through the activation of suspended sentences and deprivation of liberty for substantial periods in custody.

In order to make this reparation, offenders have an effective desert claim that the means of doing so will be available and supervised; that what is expected of them is strictly purposeful and within their capabilities; that it is of amenity value to communities, and that once it is completed the offenders concerned will be restored to full citizenship status.[8]

Crime committed within communities, while disruptive and destructive of relationships, is a matter requiring the consideration of both social and criminal justice. It is a social phenomenon that goes beyond the narrower definitions of laws, of law breaking and the reciprocal punishment of offenders because its dysfunctional nature affects a wider spectrum of legitimate interests. Dealing appropriately with crime within communities is but one

8 This also brings into discussion the question of whether, when offenders have satisfied the conditions and reparative requirements of community sanctions, the offences for which the sanctions were imposed should be regarded as 'spent' after a period of time and not taken into account as previous convictions on any future sentencing occasion.

important component of social justice,[9] whereas criminal law is the means of focusing opprobrium upon those alone who transgress its provisions.

Within a predominantly retributive framework of criminal justice, the dominant focus is placed on past events and what offenders 'deserve' in relation to the seriousness of their offences. This emphasis and the conditions in which it is applied are not conducive to behavioural change or 'correction' in either the custodial or non-custodial sectors of criminal justice, since its retrospective focus largely denies offenders the opportunity to examine the causes of their wrongdoing, to take responsibility for it, or to make amends for it through victim reparation. These opportunities are, as we have noted previously, a legitimate desert claim for all of the stakeholders within the criminal justice process, and provide a potentially prospective purpose for it that is significantly lacking at present.

The Crime and the Victim Perspective

To make matters worse, there is under present circumstances no particular expectation that offenders should accept responsibility (guilt) for their behaviour or make reparation to victims. It is left to the prosecution authorities to prove the guilt of offenders at trials which are often and unnecessarily extended in duration by the entry of 'not guilty' pleas which are tacitly encouraged by less than scrupulous defence lawyers.[10]

Victims are all too frequently the casualties of criminal acts which can have a traumatising and long-lasting effect upon their lives either physically or psychologically (or both). Many victims who may also be prosecution witnesses find court proceedings intimidating and difficult to understand in procedural terms, and very stressful when they become subject to cross-examination of an aggressive nature. It remains, therefore, extraordinary that, in spite of repeated promises to afford them greater consideration within the justice process, they remain almost marginalised bystanders apart from when they are needed for their potential value as witnesses.

We have noted earlier in this work (in Chapter 9) some of the potential hazards inherent in the involvement of victims and offenders within mediation processes stemming from the dangers of intimidation, further traumatisation and distress. Although the procedure for enabling victims to submit victim impact statements (VISs) or victim personal statements (VPSs) expressing their situations to the courts is an avenue by which this situation has been significantly improved and has been outlined in the course of this study,

9 Other components of social justice include the equitable distribution of wealth, opportunity and access to amenities, the upholding of rights and freedoms, and the protection of privacy and religious expression.

10 On the basis that the prosecution may have insufficient evidence to prove the charge, that doubt may be cast on the nature or reliability of the evidence, or that the accused may be acquitted on a legal technicality.

their actual legal status and entitlement to redress remain unsatisfactorily defined within England and Wales law.[11]

It is also a frequently overlooked fact that the immediate dependents of offenders can become coincidental victims of the criminal justice process, particularly in instances in which unnecessary overuse of imprisonment occurs. Genuine hardship often arises when parents or carers of young persons are imprisoned and families are left without the major wage earner and become dependent upon social benefit support (Ministry of Justice, 2012c).

Communities as Victims of Crime

High rates of crime and re-offending within communities disrupt the social environment and provoke a fear of victimisation within them. This in turn leads to the migration of law-abiding families to other areas, depression of housing values, reduction in social amenities, lack of business investment, high rates of vandalism and a strain on policing

11 Here it will be noted that there are historical reasons for this situation that require explanation, since the United Kingdom stands almost alone among European countries in its relationship with the legal requirements of membership of the European Union. The UK is a signatory to the Treaty on European Union (Maastricht) 1992, which established the European Parliament, the EU Council, the European Commission and the European Court of Justice, and the Treaties of Amsterdam (1997), of Nice (2000) and of Lisbon (2007), each of which had legal implications binding upon member countries. The Amsterdam Treaty (1997) created the legal basis of EU Council Framework Decisions, which in turn enabled the Framework Decision of 15 March 2001 [2001/220/JHA] on the standing of victims in criminal proceedings (OJ L 82, 22.3.2001) that established basic rights for victims of crime within the EU, and required Member States to adapt their legislation in line with the requirements of the framework decision by 2006. The response to this decision was variable across the Member States, and in 2009 it was concluded that the legislation had been ineffective in achieving minimum rights for victims across the EU.
Meanwhile, the Treaty of Lisbon (2007) had abolished framework decisions in favour of EU directives and regulations binding upon Member States for compliance, and in 2012 EU Directive 2012/29/EU establishing minimum standards on the rights, support and protection of victims of crime (aka Brussels 2011) was adopted and effective from 15 November 2012, and required Member States to implement its provisions into their national laws by 16 November 2015. To this end, DG Justice and the Commission issued a guidance document to assist compliance and enactment (European Commission, DG Justice, 2013 – Ref: Ares (2013)3763804-19/12/2013).
However, in October 2012 the government of the United Kingdom negotiated an opt-out derogation agreement with the EU in matters relating to legal provisions (unless opting-in on a voluntary basis became preferable) effective from 1 December 2014, by which means compliance with the former framework decisions and subsequent EU directives became optional and a matter of national decision in terms of compliance. This accounts to a significant extent for the failure of the UK to implement the EU minimum standards in relation to the treatment of victims of crime to this time, since to do so would have both structural and financial implications in requiring significant reform of the penal system and its associated legislative provisions. This remains the case in spite of numerous government documents issued since 1996 purporting to acknowledge the need for adequate victim recognition (Home Office 1996; 2003b; 2005a; b; c; and d; and Ministry of Justice 2012. See also: http://ec.europa.eu/justice/criminal/victims/rights/index_en.htm (Accessed 13 April 2015).

resources. Such areas become known as undesirable places in which to live or work, while at the same time they generate a deviant subculture favourable to the formation of gangs and a 'normalisation' of delinquent and anti-social behaviour.

On the other hand, socially cohesive communities in which crime is less frequent and seriously deplored offer mutual support to their inhabitants which inhibits and discourages offending. In such areas it is perceived as appropriate that offenders should make amends and reparation to both victims and the community as a means of being restored to community status. These communities generate stable and harmonious environments that are inclusive of all their inhabitants without discrimination, and in which it is difficult for delinquency to flourish without being immediately evident and confronted. In such areas the need for frequent and high-profile policing is minimal since both the likelihood of crime detection and normative standards of behaviour are high.

Many Western European countries have suffered similarly from the generation of high-density urban housing estates on the fringes of cities to accommodate both native and immigrant populations seeking employment close to the opportunities for education, employment and recreational amenities. It is into these urban estates that many predominantly younger people from rural communities seeking the same opportunities and amenities have also moved, but without the need to rely upon the lesser frequency of public transportation services or the relatively high costs of private travel. It is difficult for such urban concentrations to generate a community ethos when accommodation changes hands frequently and many inhabitants do not know or socialise with even their next-door neighbours. Such an atmosphere of impersonality and comparative social isolation has also proved to be conducive to the development of delinquent subcultures in which it is easier for criminals to avoid detection.

Where Does This Analysis Lead?

Within the scope of this chapter an attempt has been made to indicate and explain why the 'traditional' and hitherto widely accepted retributive and retrospective notion of desert within criminal punishment presents only a partial and limiting interpretation of its true importance within contemporary penology. No attempt has been made to deny the fact that criminal offending should have serious consequences, but rather to suggest that such is only one component of a much more comprehensive interpretation of what desert consists in, and that it can have a prospective and much more useful contemporary purpose.

As the title of this work suggests, the concept of reparation has the potential to transform the criminal justice process within a prospective framework with far wider social benefit than the solely retrospective approach allows. Far from being exclusive, as the traditional justification has proved to be, the reparative framework is essentially inclusive of offenders, victims and communities all of whom have, to some or another extent, become the casualties of the historical explanation.

In concluding this chapter, it is necessary to provide some explanation of how the proposal for reparative prisons and the regimes they might operate could work in a positive manner to reduce pressure on the custodial penal system while at the same time contributing to a reduction in post-custody recidivism. It will have been noted that the segment of the prison population identified as being potentially suitable for these regimes involved primarily those offenders sentenced to four years or less with an effective custody period of two years or less. It was further suggested that where availability of places allows, it might be advantageous to include in these regimes selected offenders serving longer sentences who are within the final two years of their effective sentence periods.

Regime Design

In terms of security provision, these prisons would be of a closed nature but in a lesser security category than the existing long-term maximum security status of the existing 'dispersal' prisons within England and Wales. Ideally, day-to-day security and control would be operated on the now well-established 'direct supervision' model of operation[12] which is less staff intensive than that normally associated with traditional closed prisons of medium and higher security status.

The daily regime should be designed to provide a full eight-hour working day in which inmates are engaged in purposeful training and/or productive work, including remedial education where necessary, in purpose-designed workshops and horticultural areas for making saleable products for the external market or for use within the prison. Training (other than remedial education) should be of a vocational nature to equip inmates with employment and wage-earning skills upon release, and to standards of proficiency demanded within the external community.[13]

Full compliance with regime rules and behavioural requirements are a mandatory feature of the regime and rigorously enforced. Meals are taken together and food is prepared within the prison by inmates, under catering industry training conditions with professional staff supervision, as another way of acquiring certified skills. Failure to comply with regime requirements, *i.e.* 'house rules', or disruptive behaviour is confronted on a 'three strikes'

12 This model was pioneered in the USA and has been adopted by a number of other countries worldwide including South Africa where it was successfully implemented in the design and operation of the 3,000 place Mangaung Correctional Centre at Bloemfontein in the Free State. The author was operations adviser to the management of the prison during the commissioning and staff training phases of its development, including the first two years of full capacity operation.

13 These normally include trade skills associated with the construction and manufacturing industries, IT-based competencies, horticulture and rural land and environmental management.

basis involving verbal and written warnings followed, where necessary, by transfer back to traditional prison custody. Inmates accepted for reparative regime prisons therefore have much to lose if they fail to comply fully with the behavioural or regime requirements of the establishment.

Reparative prisons should also be drug-free facilities as an essential condition of participation to which those selected must provide written agreement of acceptance prior to admission. Any involvement in the use or possession of drugs within the establishment should result in immediate removal without further warning. Smoking should also be limited to outdoor (exercise) areas only, and cell accommodation be kept 'smoke free' at all times. Prison staff and employees should also be required to refrain from smoking within the perimeter of the establishment while on duty.

'Seamless' Sentence Considerations

Reparative sentences involving periods of prison custody should be viewed as progressive in nature, and with an evident link between the effective custodial period and a transitional period spent under temporary day-release conditions within communities prior to conditional release. The purpose of this concept is to provide offenders with a statutory period within the sentence during which they are 'on trial' working within communities, though returning to custody overnight. Figure 10.3 illustrates the comparison of this concept with the present release arrangement for prisoners serving sentences of up to four years imprisonment.

In relation to Figure 10.3, it should be noted that prisoners presently serving four years or more have different sentence conditions from those noted above. Between the mid-point of sentence and the two-thirds point they may be retained in prison or be granted DCR, followed by a period of ACR up to the three-quarters point before being released unconditionally (on AUR) thereafter. The arrangement proposed here does away with AUR in favour of extending the period spent under licence supervision in the community (ACR) until the sentence expiry date of four years, and as a potential means of reducing post-release recidivism.[14]

14 In relation to the illustration of sentences in Figure 10.3, the periods of sentence shown indicate the provisions for a four-year sentence. For shorter sentences, the periods of one-third, one half, and two-thirds of the relevant total sentence length would become proportionately reduced.

Figure 10.3 Present sentence conditions – prisoners serving over twelve months up to four years

Months of sentence		
0 12	24	36 48
Effective sentence period in prison custody	Automatic conditional release* (ACR)	Automatic unconditional release (AUR)

Proposed sentence conditions – Reparative sentences up to and including four years

Months of sentence			
0 12	18	24	36 48
'Effective sentence period' in prison custody or on DDR**		Non-custodial sentence period	
Mandatory prison custody	Prison custody or discretionary day release (DDR)**	Discretionary conditional release (DCR)*	Automatic conditional release* (ACR)

Notes:
* = On licence under supervision
** = On temporary day release from custody

Provision for DDR requiring prisoners to return to custody overnight would involve reparative prisons in providing secure separate accommodation for these inmates on a 'hostel' basis. This would remove the potential for 'cross-contamination' between them and those remaining in full-time custody who might use them as a means of importing unauthorised articles into the establishment.

In Chapter 11, we shall examine the requirement for enhanced community involvement in the reparative Justice Model, and in Chapter 12 conclusions will be drawn from this study as a whole and matched against the strategic aims set out in Chapter 8.

11 Community Involvement

Blueprints for Action: Community Justice Forums

If the proposals for penal reform advanced in this work are to stand any possibility of implementation, then the key to success will lie as much with communities as with a political initiative to carry them forward. Without active community involvement in criminal justice it is unlikely that policymakers, judiciaries and the government agencies responsible for justice administration will respond to the requirements for, and challenges of, strategic change.

Blueprints for community involvement are evident or emerging in other jurisdictions, most notably in Canada since the early years of this millennium (Mirsky, 2005), and in Scotland (Scottish Government, 2013; Criminal Justice Voluntary Sector Forum, 2014) more recently. This means that the task does not have to be approached on a 'first principles' or 'blank tablet' basis, and this is advantageous. The Canadian document is particularly informative as to the process by which community forums could and have been be brought into active participation in justice, and the Scottish documents set out the detailed consultative process necessary to provide strategic structure, purpose and participation.

Figure 11.1 provides a hybrid illustration of the participative structure of a community justice forum derived from the accounts previously identified.

Figure 11.1 Community Justice Forum Composition

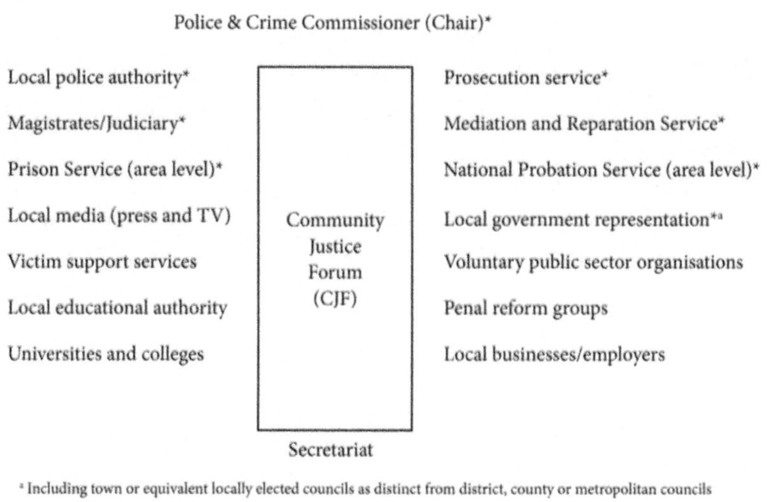

[a] Including town or equivalent locally elected councils as distinct from district, county or metropolitan councils forming part of the statutory framework of Local Government in England and Wales.

As the figure indicates, the number of parties potentially interested in the work of CJFs is widely spread in terms of appropriate representation. A careful balance would therefore need to be struck between accommodating all of these legitimate interests and not allowing the total representation to make the work of a CJF unmanageable. It might therefore be prudent to establish inner councils with permanent members to determine and direct strategic policy issues, subject to the overall approval of the full CJF membership at meetings of lesser frequency. Possible inner council membership is indicated by the asterisk (*) shown against the members concerned.

Most organisations of the nature described here devolve specific sectors of their work to sub-committees tasked with the more detailed interpretation and development of strategic aims into working policies and practices. The former Advisory Council on the Penal System mentioned in Chapter 7 worked successfully in this manner. Once again, it is advisable to keep these sub-committees to as limited a number as possible, consistent with giving them clear and non-overlapping remits as the focus for their work. Thus it might be suggested that community justice forums might devolve its detailed work to:

- a criminal justice sub-committee – concerned with matters pertaining to the work of those agencies directly responsible for dealing with offenders both in custody and in the community at all stages of sentences. This would involve the prison and probation services, the police, prosecution, mediation and reparation services, and the judiciary;
- a community affairs sub-committee – concerned with creation of opportunities and work placements for offenders, their supervision, and aspects of public safety inherent in an expansion of non-custodial disposals by the courts. This would involve primarily the probation and police services, voluntary public sector organisations, local businesses and employers;
- a victim support and offender dependents sub-committee – concerned with the welfare and reparation of victims, the welfare and support of offender's dependents, and particularly of the children of offenders in custody. This would involve the prison and probation services, the social services, victim support services and the local education authorities; and,
- a public relations sub-committee – concerned particularly with promoting and disseminating the purpose, policies and work of the CJF within the community, and, with the media, creation of a positive image of community corrections and the amenity value inherent in their operation. This would involve all the participant members of the CJF in terms of their contributions to its work.

The work of CJFs would require careful and rigorous evaluation as a matter of public accountability, and it is here that local universities and colleges and penal reform groups could be of considerable and invaluable assistance through social science research projects and advice. The Canadian experience clearly demonstrates the way in which this was achieved through a partnership with the Nanaimo Regional John Howard Society (NRJHS) and the Malaspina University. Indeed, the NRJHS assigns a trained coordinator to act as a mediator within the restorative conferencing process between victims and offenders at the pre-trial stage, where this is appropriate, and approved by government prosecutors and the courts.

Development of the Scottish model is still in progress, with emphasis on delivery of community justice services through local level community planning partnerships (CPPs) under the strategic direction of a new statutory body with responsibility for national direction and delivery of community justice services. How this will work eventually has yet to be finalised, though in essence it reflects many similarities to the Canadian model. Both models are predicated on the belief that ownership of, and support for, community justice has to be secured *within* local communities rather than statutorily and operationally imposed upon them. Both initiatives reflect a paradigm shift in criminal justice philosophy and delivery that is long overdue in meeting the desert claims of all the stakeholders identified in this work.

On a final note here, something needs to be said about the role of police and crime commissioners (PCCs) whose recent appointment in England and Wales has been controversial. PCCs were established under the Police Reform and Responsibility Act 2011 to head the strategic direction and accountability of the police to the public within each police force area outside London. They are elected members of the public within police and local authority areas, and their role is defined within the 2011 Act.[1] PCCs are responsible for setting the strategic direction and aims of each police force area through a police and crime plan in consultation with chief constables; for the appointment, performance, and if necessary dismissal of these officers; and for the allocation and spending of funds for policing and crime reduction. The performance of PCCs is assessed annually by a police and crime panel within each police force area, and which is responsible for monitoring their actions and decisions. In short, PCCs are accountable to the public for policing performance, and chief constables are responsible to PCCs for the performance of their forces.

It will have been noted that it is suggested that PCCs should, due to their public accountability, chair the CJF as an integral aspect of their role. This would seem to be a logical proposal since the composition and role of CJFs as proposed in this work embrace many aspects of crime reduction, and the agencies (both statutory and voluntary) that contribute to it on a local accountability basis on behalf of communities. The proposal would, however, have to be specifically incorporated into the role of PCCs as defined in the 2011 Act.

---

1 For a brief but sufficiently comprehensive explanation of the role and responsibility of police and crime commissioners see: Home Office, 2012. This document, with references to equality legislation, is available at www.gov.uk/government/uploads/system/uploads/attachment_data/file/117463/role-as-pcc.pdf (Accessed 13 March 2015).

THE SHAPE AND STRUCTURE OF COMMUNITY CORRECTIONS

If CJFs were to become the focal point of correctional services and policing within the community setting, then a new relationship would be required between the Ministry of Justice and the Home Office in England and Wales, which has responsibility for policing. The former, through the creation of NOMS, subsumes the prison and probation services, while also having a somewhat tenuous responsibility for the youth justice system overseen by the Youth Justice Board (YJB).[2] The latter has traditionally fulfilled the role of the department of state solely responsible for policing and crime prevention in addition to border control and immigration matters.

A possible structure for delivery of community corrections is indicated in Figure 11.2, illustrating the relationships between the various agencies that would bear direct responsibilities within a co-ordinated framework devolved by government to a local operational level.

Figure 11.2 Proposed Structure for Community Corrections

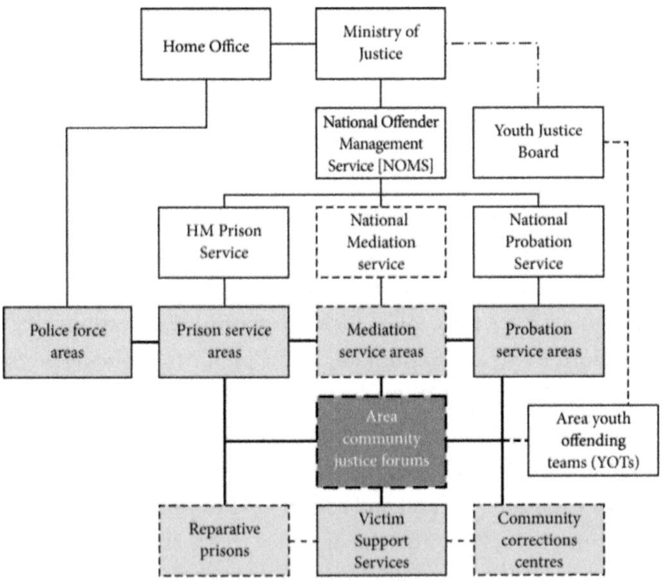

* Note: Organisations within broken line boxes are proposed in this work.

2 The YJB is an executive non-departmental public body created under the Crime and Disorder Act 1998. Its twelve members are now appointed by the justice secretary, and it operates in conjunction with the MoJ, the Department for Children, Schools and Families, and to a now more limited extent the Home Office which was its former (pre-2007) sponsor. For a more comprehensive explanation of these arrangements and the youth justice system see the very concise account in Gibson, 2009: pp. 179-181.

From the above diagram it will be noted that the proposed area criminal justice forums, with their additional membership from local government, civic and other organisations formerly described, should ideally operate with geographical boundaries that are coterminous with those of the police, prison, mediation and probation service areas. It might also be appropriate for area youth offending teams to be considered for inclusion within CJF membership, although the provisions of the youth court determine the protocols for the sanctioning of juveniles (up to 15 years of age) outside the mainstream criminal justice system.[3]

Delivery of the Crime Reduction Strategy

Within the concept of community corrections envisaged within this work to meet the desert claims of all the stakeholders in criminal justice, it would fall to area CJFs to devise a crime reduction and public safety support strategy for the area. This strategy would necessarily include, but not be limited to, meeting the following purposes:

- active participation and assistance in delivery of the police and crime plan devised between PCCs and chief constables in accordance with the provisions within the police reform and social responsibility act 2011;
- support of the area probation service in the operation of community correction centres (CCCs) to enhance public confidence in the enforcement and completion of community-based sanctions imposed on offenders by the courts;
- support of the purposes of reparative prisons in reducing post-release recidivism through the training and employment of offenders on temporary release to work on community projects in reparation of victims of crime, and their eventual resettlement within their communities;
- active support of crime victims within area communities through the provision and delivery of victim support services operated by volunteer groups with professional counselling assistance and sponsored by the national mediation and reparation service (NMRS);
- through liaison with educational and social work agencies to assist where necessary the dependents of offenders adversely affected by the absence of parents in custody; and,

3 Provisions for youth justice administration operate separately from the mainstream criminal justice system under the provisions of the Crime and Disorder Act 1998 and subsequent legislation. Youth offending teams (YOTs) operate in close liaison with local youth offending panels (YOPs) which are statutory local panels, and police working under the auspices of YOTs (see: Gibson, 2009: 180-181).

- involvement of the local media within CJF areas in the creation of a positive image of community corrections and policing as a means of enhancing public confidence in the effectiveness of the criminal justice and crime prevention processes.

If these purposes could be met and communicated to the public on an annual basis, then CJFs would have made a much-needed and socially valuable contribution to the welfare and wellbeing of community relations and the reduction of crime on a national basis.

Community Corrections Centres (CCCs)

From that which has been suggested above it will be evident that the creation and operation of community correction centres is pivotal to the effectiveness of the non-custodial criminal justice process of the future in England and Wales and in other democracies. Public confidence in this effectiveness is a critical issue in crime reduction, and one which simply cannot be overlooked. This confidence in turn depends upon community corrections being perceived as having a significant potential to reduce both offending and re-offending, while at the same time repairing the social harm caused by crime and making communities safer places to live in. This, in essence, is what CCCs must demonstrably achieve.

It is, without doubt, a matter of debate whether the existing National Probation Service, with its historic legacy and social work ethos over more than a century, could sustain a further and possibly turbulent reincarnation in its present form. Indeed, its original 'caring, befriending and assisting' image has been significantly modified in recent decades into one of 'managerial instrumentalism' by which offenders within communities are subject to 'compliance surveillance' for the duration of non-custodial sanctions, but the causes of their criminality and remedial measures are no longer the focal issues for the service to address, even if the necessary resources of time and casework intensity were available to do so.

Such may seem a harsh judgement of a service that has constantly and professionally struggled to meet the changing expectations made of its members over the past two decades in particular. For as Robinson and McNeill (2003) indicated in a related context, there has been a deliberate 'repositioning' of probation within the criminal justice process since the late 1990s. This change of emphasis has been evident in an attempted managerial re-alignment of the relationship between the prison and probation services within NOMS, traditionally a fragile professional relationship at best, in pursuit of an elevation of community sanctions from below the 'custody threshold' to a status of almost equivalent 'penal bite' with that of short custodial sentences. Also, and of equal importance, the change was made in an attempt to persuade the courts to make lesser use of the latter. Unfortunately, as we have seen in this work, the courts did not 'buy into' the equivalence notion, and persisted with widespread use of short-term prison custody as a preferred option.

All of this stated, however, the establishment of CCCs could retrieve this situation, but this would imply a further and considerable re-alignment of the National Probation Service role into that of a dedicated correctional services agency with a sanction-enforcement role within which the changing of offending behaviour would depend to a significant extent upon mediation and victim reparation rather than upon individual casework intervention alone. However, given the known and acknowledged desert claim of offenders to assistance in overcoming their social deficits, this would imply a balancing of these imperatives within the revised structure of community-based sanctions.

Achieving this balance would need to be 'designed into' the role and purpose of CCCs in a deliberate and demonstrable manner if a reduction in post-sanction recidivism were to be accepted as the primary objective of their operation. Thus the nature and design of crime correction centres premises and their staffing would become issues of considerable importance. Situated within local communities, these facilities would require a secured perimeter within which both vocational training and offending behaviour programmes could be accommodated with the necessary support facilities for effective delivery of each on a campus basis and in a disciplined environment.

Vocational training should be confined to imparting sufficient practical skills to enable offenders to participate effectively in community amenity projects proposed to and approved by the CJF, and supervised by trained CCC staff with the assistance of local community representatives or employers. Delivery of offending behaviour programmes would require the employment of professionally accredited facilitators who would become community correctional service employees.

The success of CCCs within the community would heavily depend upon the demonstrable effectiveness of their amenity enhancing function and disciplined approach to project management and delivery. This would necessitate the evident presence of offenders working on projects under sensitive supervision, and without exposing offenders to harassment or ridicule by community members. For these reasons, allocation of offenders to menial tasks such as litter clearing, refuse disposal and graffiti removal should be avoided in favour of constructive tasks enhancing the environment of the community and its leisure activities. CCCs might also capitalise on tasks of rural and environmental value where local authorities presently lack the funding or manpower to maintain or improve rights of way, woodlands, parks, waterways, and the like.

In order to meet the commitments to victim reparation and also the reduction of recidivism through adoption of normal and law-abiding lifestyles, offenders should be paid realistic wages from which deductions for victim reparation could be made at source. Wages should therefore be paid to national minimum wage levels at least, with suitable increments for skilled work where accredited employment skills are achieved and used.

Provision of appropriate midday food both within the CCC campus and available to parties working in the wider community[4] would also become a necessary logistical function of CCC operation.

From the brief explanation offered above it will be evident that the role and operation of CCCs envisaged here is of a comprehensive nature that would require a deliberate infrastructural investment, while at the same time requiring the establishment of a disciplined community corrections service functioning in tandem with the reparative prisons sector of the Prison Service. It could be funded to a very considerable extent by reductions in the size and extent of the prison population and also of the custodial Prison Service estate, while also increasing community involvement and victim reparation within the criminal justice process.

Above all of these considerations, the proposals advanced here demonstrate with clarity how, and to what extent, a comprehensive re-appraisal and restatement of the concept of desert within criminal justice has become both necessary and desirable in the contemporary interpretation of correctional theory and practice. The proposals also highlight how the legitimate desert claims of all the parties to, and stakeholders in, criminal justice can be effectively accommodated.

The proposals do, however, leave the future role and ethos of the existing National Probation Service as a matter of considerable debate. It is questionable whether, given the traditional nature of its title and distinguished history, the supervision of offenders subject to community rehabilitation orders[5] and other generic community sentences imposed by the courts conveys an accurate description of its contemporary role within either society or the criminal justice process. The term community correctional services suggested here subsumes the wider context of the work presently performed by the National Probation Service which has itself experienced a considerable extent of internal reorganisation and reshaping from 2002 onwards (see: Gibson, 2009: 132-133). The most recent development in this respect has been the initiative of government to outsource certain former National Probation Service tasks such as the post-release supervision of former prisoners to the private sector, a move which has been widely criticised within and beyond the National Probation Service itself.

The questions that overarch all of these considerations concern who the primary customers of the criminal justice process actually are, and what these customers are entitled to expect in terms of service. Put another way, what is it that the customers deserve in return for their investment in the criminal justice process as stakeholders? The answer

4 Possibly in the form of packed lunches or heated container meals delivered by CCC transport to project locations on a daily basis.

5 Formerly probation orders which were replaced by the description community rehabilitation orders in § 43 of the Criminal Justice and Court Services Act 2002, the same year in which the National Probation Service assumed its new title.

would seem to be evident in the opening words of the statement of purpose of the Prison Service which stipulates: 'HM Prison Service serves the public…'. And, lest it be overlooked, it is the public who as taxpayers and predominantly law-abiding citizens also fund the enterprise, and must at the least deserve some assurance that it is as cost and outcome effective as it can be made.

In the final chapter, an attempt will be made to draw out the main threads of the discussion within this book, and what may be concluded from it concerning the future of the criminal justice process in England and Wales and elsewhere in which similar situations prevail. The reader will, however, have noted that the statistical data relating to the detailed size and composition of the prison population of England and Wales and its accommodation have changed repeatedly during the months during which this work has been prepared.[6] While every attempt has been made to update and amend these data, the overall situation remains broadly as described throughout this work.

6 This applies particularly to the data concerning the total prison population, its distribution within sentence length bands, and the accommodation levels of crowded and uncrowded occupancy available. At the time of finalisation (mid-September 2015), the overall population in prison custody had risen to almost 86,000, the In-use CNA level stands at 77,358, and thus the overcrowding factor at 8,342 or 10.78%. The latter figures do not, however, allow a 5% reduction for accommodation under repair or refurbishment, and if this were implemented, the more realistic situation would reveal a potential reduction of some 3,868 uncrowded places, thus making the more realistic overcrowding factor 17.02%.

12 Conclusions

Review of This Work

When this book was completed in September 2015, which was a general election year in Britain, there were 85,699 people held in penal custody in England and Wales (81,780 males and 3,919 females): an incarceration rate of 149 *per* hundred thousand of the population. Of the males, 84,310 are housed in prison custody, and 1,389 in Immigration Removal Centres. There are no females held in the latter form of accommodation. The usable operational capacity of prisons (crowded capacity) stands at 87,831, certified normal accommodation (CNA) at 77,358,[1] and some 2,000 offenders are on temporary release from prisons under home detention curfew (HDC) conditions.[2] The number of persons held in custody awaiting trial or sentence stands at 11,785, a slight decrease from the early months of 2015.

The central purpose of this work has been to redefine the concept of desert within criminal punishment. This redefinition has become urgently necessary because the criminal justice process in England and Wales, as in some other democracies, has become incapable of delivering crime reduction and reducing post-release recidivism to a critical extent. As matters currently stand the process is, to a considerable extent, unfit for purpose. As my colleague John Blad has previously described such situations, the process has deteriorated over time to resemble an old and failing hospital that has absorbed so many viruses that it has become pathogenically incapable of curing the sick (Blad, 2006: 135).

Probably the most pervasive of these viruses is the fact that, since the end of World War 2 and the subsequent demise of the rehabilitative ideal, considerations relating to desert within criminal punishment have focused almost exclusively upon retributive and retrospective action against offenders as the primary justification of punishment. The secondary justification for this action has been that its severity will have a measurable effect in deterring crime in offenders and others, and that when this fails to occur, the inevitable response must be to increase the amount of punishment imposed.

This has led in turn to a second virus in the virtual abandonment of proportionality in punishment – a concept which in itself is difficult to achieve between similar and different offences – and the form of penal instrumentalism that uses offenders as the means of pursuing social policy objectives beyond the reduction of crime. Thus, incapacitation of

1 But here see the reservation of considerable caution over CNA expressed in Chapter 9, p. 77, Note 17.

2 If these persons fail to abide by the conditions of their temporary release on HDC, or commit further offences, they are liable to immediate return to custody. They are not, however, counted as being held in prison custody.

offenders for increasing and in some instances indeterminate periods of time can only be justified on the basis of social protection rather than of strict punishment.

Deprivation of liberty is the most serious sanction available to the courts within most civilised democracies, and should therefore be used as a means of last resort and to the least extent possible. Its use in instances in which it is avoidable, unnecessary or counter-productive is unjustifiable, socially damaging, and wasteful of scarce and expensive resources. Such is particularly the case where overcrowding of prisons defeats the objective of promoting behavioural change and reducing post-sentence recidivism.

This study has highlighted the persistent overuse of short prison sentences rather than the wider use of non-custodial sanctions in England and Wales despite repeated advice to governments through reputable research findings and the conclusions of inquiries (*e.g.* Wiegend, 2001; Home Office, 2001; Esmeé Fairbairn Foundation, 2004a[3] and b) that such sentences fail to reduce recidivism and may actually encourage it. To make matters worse, overcrowded prisons are largely incapable of delivering regimes that address the causes of offending behaviour for short-sentence prisoners, and the present extent of overcrowding has been clearly indicated within this work. It has therefore been concluded that the case for abandoning such sentences in favour of community penalties other than in exceptional instances is compelling.

The principle of parsimony in sentencing also has an important role within these considerations. Because the practice of punishment inevitably results in the imposition of unpleasant consequences upon offenders, the principle insists that this should be restricted to the least extent consistent with the seriousness of offences that have been committed. Punishment over and above this extent, or imposed for purposes other than marking offence gravity and culpability,[4] becomes an excessive and instrumental use of state power over citizens. It also calls into question the entire notion of desert where this is confined to considerations of retributive punishment alone. This is the third virus that has infected the criminal justice process over the past two decades in particular.

Such is not to suggest that wrongdoing should not have consequences in the form of sanctions or punishments for those who commit offences that breach the law's provisions, or that these sanctions should not be to some evident extent commensurate with that of the harm caused by the wrongdoing which may reasonably be considered as deserved. But this calculus will inevitably be of an imprecise nature within and between offence types, which in turn suggests that the notion of proportionality can, at best, be only of an approximate nature and that the entire concept of desert requires re-definition.

---

3 The Coulsfield report into alternatives to prison (see: Cameron, 2004).

4 Such as the use of exemplary punishment for the purposes of general deterrence (instrumental punishment), or for the long-term incapacitation of those considered to pose a significant public risk of further serious re-offending. Predictions of criminal dangerousness are liable to high (over 50%) levels of false-positive outcomes (here see: Bottoms, 1977: *passim*; Cornwell, 1989: 61-66 and *passim*, and others).

The Need to Redefine Desert

Why is revision of the concept of desert so essential to the reconfiguration of the criminal justice process? Simply stated, it is indispensable because focusing criminal punishment in an entirely retributive manner upon past events (negative desert) neglects and denies the legitimate expectation that its outcomes should be prospectively beneficial to the social order (positive desert). And in order for it to be beneficial it has to meet the reasonable and positive desert claims of all of the stakeholders involved in the criminal justice process. These claims are those of victims, dependents, communities, and of offenders themselves. The law itself has no specific claim to compliance: it is, rather, the means by which non-compliance is dealt with.

Giving those with positive desert claims what is strictly due to them is an integral purpose of true justice. Neglecting to do so by focusing retributive desert exclusively upon those who offend deprives those offended against of an equitable outcome of the justice process. For centuries, criminal justice processes have been sustained by the premise that it is the state and its laws that have been the primary victim of wrongdoing: a claim which, upon examination, will be seen to be profoundly illogical, and which has been robustly challenged in this work.

Redefining the true nature of desert within this book has resulted in the identification and recognition of the various positive desert claims of all the parties to criminal offending, and placing these in a context much wider than that of the narrower traditional and retributive concept that has shaped criminal justice policies hitherto. The extent to which the latter concept has proved to be dysfunctional in its outcomes has also been explained and demonstrated. Such a redefinition has been essential to the concept of delivering more effective justice while making more constructive and purposeful use of sanctions within both the custodial and non-custodial sectors of correctional practice. In the same process, the legitimate expectations of the justice process held by victims of crime and communities who are also stakeholders have been defined and evaluated.

Within This Book

In Chapters 1 and 2 an explanation has been provided of the way in which contemporary penology has come to accept a taken-for-granted and limited relationship between the concept of desert and retributive punishment to an almost exclusive extent. This development has resulted in forms of excessively punitive policy-making behaviour which has generated persistent penal crises in many democracies through the escalation of prison populations and acceptance of exorbitant penal costs, while having limited impact upon crime rates or post-sanction re-offending. Political frustration with these developments has also led to an era of increasing penal instrumentalism through the use of criminal punishment for the pursuit of social policy objectives beyond the strictly necessary response to criminal offending.

Changing patterns in post-World War II penology in particular, which have contributed significantly to political frustration with crime, may be seen to have changed the nature of criminal justice policies away from attempts to reduce crime and towards a 'managerial' agenda to control crime. As a result, increasing emphasis has been placed on the incapacitation of escalating numbers of offenders in the claimed interests of public protection, rather than on attempting to change offending behaviour.

It also became evident that increasing attention paid by the mass media to crime promoted a form of political stalemate in which politicians of major political parties, fearful of being perceived as 'soft on crime', adopted ever more aggressive penal policies to preserve their electoral credibility, and were resistant to initiatives for criminological innovation based upon international research evidence, considered academic discourse and analysis.

In Chapter 2 the history of the development of desert philosophy was traced from its earliest recorded origins through to the post-Enlightenment Period and onwards into the present millennium. This brief study provided some fascinating insights into the developments of social and legal philosophy and jurisprudence that have contributed widely to the formation of penal policies and the conceptualisation of desert through the ages and to the present day. In particular it focused attention upon the vacuum created in correctional theory and practice by the demise of both the rehabilitative ethic during the 1970s and the 'Justice Model' of commensurate deserts which replaced it, albeit briefly, during the 1980s. These developments heralded a return to the predominantly retributive and deterrent punishment agendas adopted by Western-style governments almost universally during the 1990s and into the present millennium. It was this transition that drove desert into its entirely retributive mode, and closed off almost every other conversation about alternative explanations of desert theory.

In a deliberate attempt to re-open these conversations, Chapter 3 focused upon the relative claims of corrective, distributive and compensatory forms of justice and desert by way of contrast with that of entirely punitive retributive justice which has for too long dominated penological theory and practices. This discussion led logically to examination of the emergence of restorative justice during the 1990s in particular, and subsequently as a potentially preferable concept of justice of a utilitarian nature capable of accommodating the purposes of the three others previously mentioned.

Chapter 4 extended the discussion in the previous chapter and its algebraic formulation advanced by Celello (undated) and a number of other writers subsequently. In the course of this discussion it became possible to suggest a re-formulation of the retributively negative and backward-looking algebraic explanation into a more positive and forward-looking alternative more amenable to meeting the legitimate desert claims of all the parties to criminal offending. The principal outcome of this intriguing debate involved an analysis of the competing ethical claims of two contrasting justice paradigms – the one retributive and the other described as a reparative model – to the moral high ground of the penology of the future.

The foregoing analysis clearly indicated a situation in which contemporary criminal justice processes in many democracies have reached a crossroads at which moral and ethical choices have ultimately to be made as to which paradigm provides the preferable means of shaping justice administration in years to come. In Chapter 5 it became necessary to examine some of the main reasons why justice processes in many democracies are in or close to crisis as a direct result of pursuing predominantly retributive and incapacitative penal policies. The contemporary penal system of England and Wales provided a basis for this analysis, and for discussion of the reasons why it must be considered to be no longer fit for purpose in a modern democracy. The outcomes of this situation in terms of relative national imprisonment rates within Western Europe indicated with evident clarity the widely divergent nature of penal populations in relation to overall national populations that exist throughout these countries. The discussion somewhat inevitably led to the question of why some countries like the United Kingdom continue to absorb huge penal costs while others demonstrably do not.

At this point it was clearly apparent that if significant change was to be envisaged and a reparative Justice Model adopted as a preferred penal strategy, then it would be necessary to build a consensus to deliver that outcome. The choice of strategy would lie between measures to achieve crime control and those to achieve crime reduction through reduced recidivism and more effective sentencing policies. The traditional retributive model favoured the former, while a reparative desert espoused the latter.

In Chapter 6 it became necessary to elaborate the outline of what a reparative desert strategy would entail, and the extent of change that would thus become necessary. It was, however, important to recognise that the two models were not necessarily mutually exclusive since both might have to be accommodated within a redesigned penal system as a means of dealing appropriately with the most and the less serious forms of criminal offending

Experience of building a consensus for reform was available from the Finnish penal reform programme begun in the 1980s and which has endured effectively to the present time. It was, however, evident that reform would result in a 'dual desert' paradigm entailing a measure of penal 'bifurcation' which had proved to be a source of philosophical contention in the past for reasons that needed to be explained. Lesser use of penal custody would require a corresponding expansion of, and investment in, community-based correctional services implying some measure of additional public risk. Thus, the required consensus would necessarily involve the existing agencies of criminal justice (police, prosecution authorities, courts, judiciary, prison and probation services) together with politicians, policymakers, academics, the media and local government and community representatives.

In Chapter 7 the task of building the necessary consensus was addressed in some considerable detail based upon the Finnish experience, and the outlines of a reparative desert strategy for penal reform described in Chapter 6. This involved the identification of the key strategic institutions and government departments that must necessarily participate in the strategy design, and in particular also the judiciary with its long-standing tradition of independence from both the executive and legislative functions of government. It was also acknowledged that inclusion of the media, which in the United Kingdom has been a forceful source of criticism of penal policies and the penal process, would prove to be indispensable in creating a positive image for the reform strategy once arrived at and articulated. The role and work of the former Advisory Council on the Penal System during the 1960s and 1970s was also referred to as a positive example of consensus-based penal reform – at least to a more limited and all too short-lived extent.

Chapter 8 was devoted to a discussion of how a penal reform strategy might be evolved, definition of the strategic aims and assumptions (both philosophical and operational) upon which it might be constructed, and the strategic options that would become available for its implementation. The strategic aims were defined as:

Aim 1. To reduce and restrict the average daily prison population to a maximum level that is operationally viable without overcrowding (CNA – 5%), and to a reduced level if possible.

Aim 2. To remove the option of immediate short-term custodial sentencing from the penalty structure by replacement with demanding community sanctions combined with suspended custodial sentence provisions.

Aim 3. To maximise provision for, and use of, reparative sentencing measures in both the custodial and community settings for those offenders assessed as suitable for such regimes;

Aim 4. To reserve the traditional mode of imprisonment for serious offenders who represent a significant public risk; or who are sentenced to more than twenty-four effective months in custody; or who are deemed behaviourally unsuitable for participation in reparative regimes.

The strategic options were identified as essentially four in number including:

- selecting a desired outcome imprisonment rate *per* hundred thousand of population consistent with at least the median rate prevailing in Western Europe;
- deciding upon the desired maximum un-crowded accommodation level of the custodial prisons estate affordable in fiscal terms, and which would be ring-fenced from future over-occupation;

- determining the extent of reduction in the prison population that abandonment of short (*i.e.* twelve months or less) prison sentences would deliver in conjunction with abandonment of overcrowding, and declare this as the maximum capacity of the future prisons estate; and,
- investigating the feasibility of removing and rehousing the remand (untried and unconvicted) prison population in sufficiently secure and purpose-built accommodation geographically adjacent to the courts in which they are committed for trial.

At this stage, further debate in relation to the future size and nature of the reformed and expanded community corrections sector was left in abeyance pending a more comprehensive analysis of the requirements it would be have to meet within a reparative Justice Model of corrections, and once the overall strategy for reform had been determined and selected in terms of the strategic options identified above.

Within the same chapter it was also possible, in addition to identifying the strategic options noted above, to arrive at a set of six strategic assumptions to meet the aims of a reformed penal system and underpin delivery of these options. These were defined as follows:

Assumption A. That a consensus for reform could be formed including the agencies previously identified, and including victim support agencies.

Assumption B. That if a significant majority consensus for reform could be reached, the ministers of state heading the key strategic institutions would combine to present the proposals for reform to parliament in legislative form.

Assumption C. That the financial savings resulting from reductions in the custodial penal population and the prisons estate would be directly transferable to the expansion of community correctional services in delivery of the reform package;

Assumption D. That adoption of the reforms would necessitate the creation of a professional mediation service to work in conjunction with the police and Crown Prosecution Service in cases deemed appropriate for mediation between offenders and victims at the pre-trial stage.

Assumption E. That the reforms, if implemented, would require a considerably more integrated relationship between the prison and probation services, ideally in a unified correctional services structure within the Ministry of Justice; and,

Assumption F. That the reducing levels of recorded crime throughout Western Europe (including Britain) over the past two decades will remain a stable trend, even though Britain remains identified as a 'high-crime society' within the OECD comparative survey to 2012.

In Chapter 9 it next became necessary to provide some definition of what a Reparative Justice Model would contribute to the overall penal reform strategy, the premises upon which it would be based, and the extent to which it would meet the strategic aims and options for reform described previously. This study involved a clear description of what reparative justice consists in, how the model would be constructed, how it would satisfy the redefined nature of desert, and a somewhat detailed analysis of the existing custodial penal population by sentence length, offence group, and gender. The latter analysis was deemed necessary in order to quantify and evaluate the strategic options and assumptions identified in Chapter 8.

The analysis was also helpful in determining the proportion of the prison population serving sentences of more than twelve months and up to four years (with effective custodial periods of two years or less under current rules) that might be potential candidates for the reparative Justice Model regimes which would become central to the operation of reparative prisons envisaged within the overall penal reform strategy. These prisons would operate separately from the long-term and more 'traditional-style' prisons which would accommodate serious and longer sentenced offenders of higher security categories and custodial requirements.

In Chapter 10, bearing the title 'Putting the Pieces Together', an attempt was made to draw together all the disparate aspects and factors relating to a reparative desert concept of justice arising within the previous chapters, before turning to consider the key issue of community involvement. The dominant focus upon the penal process to this point had necessarily been upon the custodial penal population since the necessity for its reduction concerned three of the four strategic aims of the reform strategy. In addition, the overcrowded conditions in which penal custody was (and still is) administered had to be overhauled and delimited if the reform strategy was to stand a chance of success, and reparative prisons were to become a reality.

Chapter 11 was entirely devoted to sketching a blueprint for community corrections based upon the concept of Community Justice Forums (CJFs), their composition and operation, and their potential to meet Strategic Aim 3 of the reform strategy. A proposed structure for community correctional services was described, and the links with reparative prisons identified. The establishment and operation of community corrections centres (CCCs) was also discussed, since these facilities would become of crucial importance to enhanced public confidence in the effectiveness of the reformed criminal justice process.

Proposals were also advanced for the development of a National Mediation and Reparation Service (NMRS) as an agency within the Ministry of Justice to coordinate and sponsor the work of voluntary sector victim support services augmented by professional counselling support. The NMRS would also administer the financial proceeds of reparation project work by offenders for the compensation of victims of crime and their dependents on an area basis.

In the final part of Chapter 11, the difficult issue of the role of the existing National Probation Service and its relationship with the Prison Service and reparative prisons within community corrections was identified. It is a sensitive issue of differing professional philosophies and ethos that can only be resolved on a cooperative basis, and possibly by the creation of a unified correctional services structure within the Ministry of Justice and NOMS, capable of accommodating the differing but in many respects contiguous roles of these two important public service organisations. Both have a potentially vital part to play in the effective operation of CCCs, building public confidence in reshaped community corrections, and in facilitating the reduction both of overall crime and recidivism. Space in this work precluded a more detailed study of this important issue deserving of debate in a much wider forum.

On a Final Note

This book was conceived to examine the implications of reconfiguring the concept of desert within criminal justice away from its traditional retributive pre-occupation and towards a more comprehensive image of inclusive and equitable justice delivery. It has proved to be a journey along the path of which there was always a clear but distant horizon, but yet the surface of the path was stony and its borders ill defined.

Progress along this path, mostly uphill, was frequently obstructed by obstacles resistant to clearance and embedded in its surface by the passage of time. At other times, progress became easier and the signage more definitive. Such is the nature of journeys of exploration frequently encountered within criminological research in which fogs and mists are abundant, fellow travellers are only intermittently encountered, but the demons of traditionalism seem vociferous in the hedges and ditches confining the direction of travel.

This journey has been to a place where justice might be more purposeful, equitable, inclusive and understandable, but it might yet display imperfections. Its starting point was a place where justice is stagnant, its inhabitants seemingly indifferent about the viruses that infect its swamps, and content to refrain from draining these because to do so would involve discomfort. I trust that I may have found this new place or at least some image of it, but I am conscious that I may never reside there.

It remains for the reader of this work to consider and decide whether or not the argument advanced for a restatement of desert within criminal justice has been essential to the prospect of reconfiguring the penal process in a more positive and inclusive manner, and to the benefit of all of its stakeholders. Above all else, perhaps, lies the question of whether it has met the four strategic aims for reform set out in Chapter 8 and reiterated in this concluding chapter.

It seems altogether appropriate to conclude this work with a quotation of singular wisdom from that of Lode Walgrave who wrote the Foreword to this book:

> Socio-ethical arguments have been advanced as to why a restorative apriorism is more desirable than the currently predominant retributive apriorism; experience and empirical data also show that systematically giving priority to restorative responses to crime is a realistic option. The next step is to propose how a maximalist restorative justice concept could take shape in a constitutional democracy. Such an exercise abandons the safe field of imagination and enters the real world of institutions. (Walgrave, 2008: 138)

Bibliography

Acton, H.B., (Ed.), *The Philosophy of Punishment: A Collection of Papers*, London: Macmillan, 1969.

Aebi, M. & Delgrande, N., *Council of Europe Annual Penal Statistics: Survey 2012*, Strasbourg: Council of Europe, 2014.

American Friends Service Committee, *Struggle for Justice*, New York: Hill and Wang, 1972.

Aquinas, T. *Summa Theologiae*, 1274 unfinished, Benziger Brothers Edition, [tr. Fathers of the English Dominican Province], Perrysberg, Ohio: ClearSpace Publishing, 2015.

Aristotle, *The Nicomachean Ethics*, [tr. T. Irwin], Indianapolis: Hackett, 1999.

Armitage, D., *Rethinking the Foundations of Modern Political Thought*, Cambridge: Cambridge University Press, 2012, pp. 59-74.

Armstrong, K.G., 'The Retributivist Hits Back', in H.B. Acton (Ed.), *The Philosophy of Punishment: A Collection of Papers*, London: Macmillan, 1969, pp. 138-158.

Atkinson, D., 'The What Works Debate: Keeping a Human Perspective', in *Probation Journal*, Vol. 51, No. 3, 2004, pp. 248-252.

Augustine, A., 'De Civitate Dei' [tr. M. Dods], in P. Schaff (Ed.), *The Nicene and Post-Nicene Fathers*, [First Series], Vol. II, Grand Rapids: Eerdmans Publishing Company, 1956.

Bean, P., *Punishment: A Philosophical and Criminological Inquiry*, Oxford: Martin Robertson, 1981.

Beccaria, C., *Dei Delitti e Della Pene*, [English translation 'On Crimes and Punishment'], (1764), [tr. H. Paolucci], London: R. Bell, 1778, reprinted Indianapolis: Bobbs Merrill, 1963.

Becker, H.S., *Outsiders: Studies in the Sociology of Deviance*, Glencoe: Illinois Free Press, 1963.

Bedau, P., 'Retribution and the Theory of Punishment, in *Journal of Philosophy*, 75, 1978, pp. 601-620.

Bedau, H.A. & Kelly, E., 'Punishment', in *Stanford Encyclopedia of Philosophy*, at: http://Plato.stanford.Edu/entries/punishment/, 2010, (Accessed 21 November 2014).

Benn, S.I., 'An Approach to the Problems of Punishment', in *Philosophy*, 33, 1958, pp. 325-341.

Benn, S.I. & Peters, R.S., *Social Principles of the Democratic State*, London: George Allen and Unwin, 1958.

Bentham, J., *Introduction to the Principles of Morals and Legislation*, Oxford: Clarendon Press, 1780 and 1789.

Blad, J.R., 'The Seductiveness of Punishment and the Case for Restorative Justice: The Netherlands', in D.J. Cornwell (Ed.), *Criminal punishment and Restorative Justice: Past, Present and Future Perspectives*, Winchester: Waterside Press, 2006, pp. 135-148.

Blad, J.R., 'Strafrecht, Herstelrecht en Genade', in *Tijdschrift voor Herstelrecht*, 2015 (15) 1, The Hague: Boom Lemma uitgevers, 2015, pp. 68-73.

Blom-Cooper, L., 'Crime and Justice: A Shift in Perspective', in D.J. Cornwell, J.R. Blad & M. Wright (Eds.), *Civilising Criminal justice: An International Restorative Agenda for Penal reform*, Hook, Hampshire: Waterside Press, 2013, pp. 151-170.

Bosanquet, B., *Some Suggestions in Ethics*, London: Macmillan, 1918.

Bottomley, A.K., *Criminology in Focus*, London: Martin Robertson, 1979.

Bottoms, A.E., 'Reflections on the Renaissance of Dangerousness', in *Howard Journal of Criminal justice*, Vol. xvi, No. 2, 1977, pp. 70-96.

Bottoms, A.E., 'The Politics of Sentencing Reform', in C. Clarkson & R. Morgan (Eds.), *The Philosophy and Politics of Punishment and Sentencing*, Oxford: Oxford University Press, 1995, pp. 17-49.

Bottoms, A.E., Rex, S. & Robinson, G. (Eds.), *Alternatives to Prison: Options for an Insecure Society*, Devon: Willan Publishing, 2004.

Box, S., *Deterrence, Reality and Society*, London: Holt, Reinhart and Winston, 1981.

Bradley, F.H., *Ethical Studies*, Oxford: Oxford University Press, 1876.

Braithwaite, J., 'Survey Article: Repentance Rituals and Restorative Justice', in *Journal of Political Philosophy*, 8(1), 2000, pp. 115-131.

Braithwaite, J., 'Between Proportionality and Impunity: Confrontation, Truth, Prevention', in *Criminology*, 43(2), 2005, pp. 283-306.

Brink, D., 'Mill's Moral and Political Philosophy', in E.N. Zolta (Ed.), *The Stanford Encyclopedia of Philosophy*, Fall edition, 2014, available in URL format at: http://Plato.stanford.Edu/fall2014/entries/Mill-moral-political (Accessed 26 November 2014).

British Broadcasting Corporation, *World Prison Populations - UK and Western Europe*, 2014, at: http://news.bbc.co.uk/1/shared/spl/hi/uk/06/prisons/html/nn1page1.stm (Accessed 6 January 2015).

Brown, J., 'The Role of Apology in Negotiation', in *Marquette Law Review*, 87, 2001, pp. 665-673.

Brunk, C., 'Restorative Justice and the Philosophical Theories of Criminal Punishment', in M. Hadley (Ed.), *The Spiritual Roots of Restorative Justice*, Albany: State University of New York Free Press, 2001, pp. 31-56.

Cameron, J.T.C., *Crime, Courts and Confidence: Report of an Independent Inquiry into Alternatives to Prison*, London: Esmeé Fairbairn Foundation, 2004.

Cavadino, M. & Dignan, J., *The Penal System: An Introduction*, London: SAGE Publications, 1997.

Cayley, D., *The Expanding Prison: The Crisis in Crime and Punishment and the Search for Alternatives*, Toronto, Canada: House of Anasi Press, 1998.

Celello, P., 'Desert', in *Internet Encyclopedia of Philosophy*, available at: www.iep.utm.Edu/desert/Undated (Accessed 6 August 2015).

Civitas, *Comparisons of Crime in OECD Countries*, London: Institute for the Study of Civil Society, 2012.

Collins English Dictionary, P. Hanks (Ed.), London and Glasgow: Collins Publications, 1979.

Cornwell, D.J., *Criminal Dangerousness and its Punishment: Beyond the Phenomenological Illusion*, York: University of York, 1989.

Cornwell, D.J., *Criminal punishment and Restorative Justice: Past, Present and Future Perspectives*, Winchester: Waterside Press, 2006.

Cornwell, D.J., *Doing Justice Better: The Politics of Restorative Justice*, Winchester: Waterside Press, 2007.

Cornwell, D.J., *The Penal Crisis and the Clapham Omnibus: Questions and Answers in Restorative Justice*, Hampshire: Waterside Press, 2009.

Cornwell, D.J., 'Reparatieve en herstelgerichte strafrechtspleging: Een goed argument voor tweesporigheid in strafrechtelijk beleid?', in *Tijdschrift voor Herstelrecht*, 2010 (10), pp. 7-20.

Cornwell, D.J., 'Justice, and Punishment: Myths, Mercy and Anglo-Saxon Attitudes', in D.J. Cornwell, J.R.Blad & M. Wright (Eds.), *Civilising Criminal Justice: An International Restorative Agenda for Penal reform*, Hampshire: Waterside Press, 2014a, pp. 49-79.

Cornwell, D.J., *Mercy: A Restorative Philosophy*, Hampshire: Waterside Press, 2014b.

Cornwell, D.J., Blad, J.R. & Wright, M. (Eds.), *Civilising Criminal Justice: An International Restorative Agenda for Penal reform*, Hampshire: Waterside Press, 2014.

Council of Europe Eurostat, *Crime Trends in Detail – Statistics in Focus 18/2013*, S. Clarke (author), European Commission, 2013, available at http://epp.eurostat.sc.europa.eu/statistics_explained/index.php/crime_trends_in_detail (Accessed 14 October 2014).

Coyle, A., 'Restorative Justice in Prisons' Paper to the *International Prison Chaplains' Association Conference (Europe)*, 2001, available at www.icpa.net (Accessed 4 May 2010).

Criminal justice Voluntary Sector Forum, *Redesigning the Community Justice System: A Policy Briefing for CJVSF Members*, 2014, available at: www.ccpsscotland.org/cjvs/wp-content/uploads/sites/4/2014/03/CJVSF-briefing-REdesigning-the-Community-Justice-Systm1.pdf (Accessed 10 October 2014).

Cummiskey, D., 'Desert and Entitlement: A Rawlsian Consequentialist Account', in *Analysis*, Vol. 47, No. 1, (January) 1987, pp. 15-19.

DiIulio, J.J., *Governing Prisons: A Comparative Study of Prison Management*, New York: Free Press, 1987.

Dodgson, C.L., *Through the Looking Glass, and What Alice Found There*, London: Macmillan and Co., 1872.

Dunbar, I. & Langdon, A., *Tough Justice: Sentencing and Penal Policies in the 1990s*, London: Blackstone, 1998.

Edgar, K. & Newell, T., *Restorative Justice in Prisons: Making It Happen*, Winchester: Waterside Press, 2006.

Eglash, A., 'Beyond Restitution: Creative Restitution', in J. Hudson & B. Galway (Eds.), *Restitution in Criminal justice*, Lexington: D.C. Heath and Company, 1977.

Esmeé Fairbairn Foundation, *Crime, Courts and Confidence, Report of an Independent Inquiry into Alternatives to Prison*, London: The Stationery Office, 2004a.

Esmeé Fairbairn Foundation, *Rethinking Crime and Punishment*, London: Beacon Press, 2004b.

European Commission, *European System of Social Indicators*, Mannheim: ZUMA Social Indicator Department, 2007.

European Commission, *DG Justice: Rights of the Victim*, [Ref: Ares (2013) 3763804-19/12/2013], Brussels: European Commission, 2013.

European Union, *Council Framework Decision of 15 March 2001 on the Standing of Victims in Criminal Proceedings*, [2001/220/JHA], Official Journal L 82, 22.3.2001, Brussels: European Union, 2001.

European Union, *Directive on the Minimum Standards on the Rights, Support and Protection of Victims of Crime*, Brussels: European Commission, 2011.

Ewing, A.C., *The Morality of Punishment*, London: Kegan Paul, Trench and Trubner, 1929.

Ewing, A.C., 'Armstrong and the Retributive Theory', in *Mind*, Vol. 72, No. 285, (January) 1963, pp. 121-4.

Falshaw, L., Friendship, C., Travers, L. & Nugent, F., *Searching for 'What Works': An Evaluation of Cognitive Skills Programmes*, Home Office Research Findings Number 206, London: Home Office, 2003, and also in *British Journal of Forensic Practice*, 6, 2004, pp. 3-13.

Feinberg, J., 'Problematic Responsibility in Law and Morals', in *Philosophical Review*, Vol. 71, No. 3, 1962, pp. 340-351.

Feinberg, J., 'The Expressive Function of Punishment', in *The Monist*, Vol. 49, No. 3, 1965, pp. 397-423, reprinted in *Doing and Deserving*, (Essays in the Theory of Responsibility), New Jersey: Princeton University Press, 1970, pp. 95-118.

Feinberg, J., 'Justice and Personal Deserts', in *Doing and Deserving*, New Jersey: Princeton University Press, 1970.

Feldman, F., 'Desert: Reconsideration of Some Received Wisdom', in *Mind*, New Series 104, No. 413, 1995 (January), pp. 63-77.

Finkelstein, C. (Ed.), *Hobbes on Law*, Aldershot: Ashgate, 2005.

Flew, A., 'The Justification of Punishment', in *Philosophy*, 29, 1954, pp. 291-307, and also *in* H.B. Acton (Ed.), *The Philosophy of Punishment: A Collection of Papers*, London: Macmillan, 1969, pp. 83-101.

France, A., *Le Lys Rouge*, Paris: Calmann-Levy, 1894.

Friedmann, W., *Law in a Changing Society*, Harmondsworth: Penguin Books, 1964.

Garland, D., *The Culture of Control: Crime and Social order in Contemporary Society*, Oxford: Oxford University Press, 2002.

Gibson, B., *The Pocket A-Z of Criminal Justice*, Hook, Hampshire, UK: Waterside Press, 2009.

Green, T.H., (1881), *Lectures on the Principles of Political Obligation*, P. Harris & J. Morrow (Eds.), Cambridge: Cambridge University Press, 1986.

Greene, J.E., *100 Great Thinkers*, London: Simon and Schuster, 1967.

Groves, R.M., 'Research on Survey Data Quality', in *Public Opinion Quarterly*, [50th Anniversary Issue], 1987, S156-72.

Hart, H.L.A., 'Punishment and the Elimination of Responsibility', L.T. Hobhouse Memorial Lecture 1962, reprinted in *Punishment and Responsibility*, Oxford: Oxford University Press, 1968.

Hart, H.L.A., 'Prolegomenon to the Principles of Punishment' in ', in *Proceedings of the Aristotelian Society*, 1959-60, pp. 1-26.

Heath, A., Fisher, S. & Smith, S., *The Globalisation of Public Opinion Research*, Working Paper Number 109, CREST Centre for Research into Elections and Social Trends, Oxford: The CREST Centre, (March) 2005, pp. 54-59.

Hegel, G.W.F., *The Philosophy of Right*, [tr. J.M. Knox], Oxford: Clarendon Press 1967.

HM Chief Inspector of Prisons, *Annual Report 2012-13*, London: The Stationery Office, 2013.

HM Prison Service, *Certified Prisoner Accommodation*, Prison Service Order 1900, Issue No. 133, London: HM Prison Service, 2001.

Hoekema, D., *Rights and Wrongs: Coercion, Punishment and the State*, Selinsgrove: Susquehanna University Press, 1986.

Home Office, *Victim's Charter: A Statement of Rights for Victims*: London: HMSO, 1990.

Home Office, *Victim's Charter: A Statement of Standards for Victims of Crime*, London: HMSO, 1996.

Home Office, *Making Punishments Work: Report of a Review of the Sentencing Framework for England and Wales*, (The Halliday Report), London: Home Office Communications Directorate, 2001.

Home Office, *Justice for All*, CM 5563, London: HMSO, 2002.

Home Office, *Restorative Justice: The Government's Strategy*, London: Home Office Communications Directorate, 2003a.

Home Office, *A New Deal for Victims and Witnesses: National Strategy to Deliver Improved Services*, London: Home Office, 2003b.

Home Office, *Victim's Rights*, London: Home Office, 2005a.

Home Office, *The Code of Practice for Victims of Crime*, London: HMSO, 2005b.

Home Office, *Re-building Lives – Supporting Victims of Crime*, CM 6705, London: HMSO, 2005c.

Home Office, *Government Proposes New Compensation Arrangements and Better Support for Victims of Crime*, 2005d, at: http://www.cjp.org.uk/news/archive/government-proposes-new-compensation-arrangements-and-better-support-arrangements-for-victims-of-crime-07-12-2005/ (Accessed 30 July 2007).

Home Office, *Prison Population Predictions 2006-2013, England and Wales*, Home Office Statistical Bulletin 11/06, London: Home Office Research, Development and Statistics Directorate, 2006.

Home Office, *Have You Got What It Takes? Your Role as Police and Crime Commissioner (PCC)*, London: Home Office, 2012.

Honderich, T., *Punishment: The Supposed Justifications*, Harmondsworth: Penguin Books, 1976.

House of Commons, *Hansard*, 23 July, c785W and Deposited Paper 2014-0327, London: House of Commons, 2007.

House of Commons, *Hansard*, 21 January, c51W, London: House of Commons, 2013.

House of Commons, *Hansard*, 25 June, c215W. London: House of Commons, 2014.

House of Commons Library, *The Abolition of Sentences of Imprisonment for Public Protection*, SN/HR/6086, London: House of Commons, 2013.

Howard League for Penal Reform, *Weekly Prison Watch*, London: Howard League, 30 January 2015, p. 1.

Hudson, B., *Justice Through Punishment: A Critique of the Justice Model of Corrections*, Basingstoke: Macmillan Education Limited, 1987.

Hume, D., *An Enquiry Concerning the Principles of Morals*, Edited and with an Introduction by J.D. Schneewind, Indianapolis, Indiana: Hackett Publishing Co. Inc., 1983.

Hutton, N., 'Sentencing Guidelines', in M. Tonry (Ed.), *Confronting Crime: Crime Control Policy Under New Labour*, Devon: Willan Publishing, 2003, pp. 112-139.

International Centre for Prison Studies (ICPS), *World Prison Brief*, Map Data, 2014, available at: www.prisonstudies.org/world-prison-brief (Accessed 1 August 2015).

Ignatieff, M., *A Just Measure of Pain: The Penitentiary in the Industrial Revolution 1750-1850*, New York: Pantheon Books, 1978.

Joutsen, M., Rahti, R. & Pölönen, P., *Criminal Justice Systems in Europe and North America - Finland*, Helsinki: Academic Bookstore, 2001.

Kant, I., *The Metaphysical Elements of Justice*, [tr. J. Ladd], Indianapolis: Hackett Publishing Company, 1999.

King, G., Murray, C.J.L., Salomon, J.A. & Tandon, A., 'Enhancing the Validity and Cross-Cultural Comparability of Measurement in Survey Research', in *American Political Science Review*, Vol. 94, 2004, pp. 101-207.

Kristjánsson, K., 'Justice, Desert and Virtue Revisited', *Social Theory and Practice*, Vol. 29, No. 1 (January), 2003, pp. 39-63.

Kyvsgaard, B., 'Penal Sanctions and the Use of Imprisonment in Denmark', in M. Tonry (Ed.), *Penal Reform in Overcrowded Times*, New York: Oxford University Press, 2001.

Lacey, N., *The Prisoners' Dilemma: Political Economy and Punishment in Contemporary Democracies*, Cambridge: Cambridge University Press, 2008.

Lappi-Seppälä, T., 'Sentencing and Punishment in Finland: The Decline of the Repressive Ideal', in M. Tonry & R.S. Frase (Eds.), *Sentencing and Sanctions in Western Countries*, New York: Oxford University Press, 2001.

Larsson P., 'Norway Prison Use Up Slightly: Community Penalty Lots', in M. Tonry & R.S. Frase (Eds.), *Sentencing and Sanctions in Western Countries*, New York: Oxford University Press, 2001.

Lauchs, M., 'Justice and Equity v. Mercy', *Proceedings of the Australian Association for Professional and Applied Ethics 12th Annual Conference, 28-30 September*, Adelaide: Australian National University, 2005.

Lewis, C., 'Trends in Crime, Victimisation and Punishment', in A.E. Bottoms, S. Rex & G. Robinson (Eds.), *Alternatives to Prison: Options for an Insecure Society*, Devon: Willan Publishing, 2004, pp. 28-58.

Lipton, D., Martinson, R. & Wilks, J., *The Effectiveness of Correctional Treatment*, London and New York: Praeger Publications, 1975.

Lynn, P., Gabler, S. & Laaksonen, S., 'Methods for Achieving Equivalence of Samples in National Surveys: The European Social Survey Experience', *Working Papers of the Institute for Social and Economic Research*, Colchester: University of Essex, 2004.

Mabbott, J.D., 'Punishment', in *Mind*, Vol. xlviii, No. 190, 1939, and also *in* H.B. Acton (Ed.), *The Philosophy of Punishment: A Collection of Papers*, London: Macmillan, 1969, pp. 39-54.

Mabbott, J.D., (1955), 'Professor Flew on Punishment', in H.B. Acton (Ed.), (1969), *The Philosophy of Punishment: A Collection of Papers*, London: Macmillan, 1969, pp. 115-129.

Martinson, R., 'What Works? Questions and Answers About Prison Reform', in *The Public Interest*, 35, (Spring), 1974, pp. 22-54.

Matza, D.M., *Becoming Deviant*, Englewood Cliffs: Prentice-Hall, 1969.

McLeod, O., 'Contemporary Interpretations of Desert: Introduction', in L. Pojman & O. McLeod (Eds.), *What Do We Deserve?A Reader on Justice and Desert*, New York: Oxford University Press, 1999, pp. 61-69 and pp. 186-195.

Merrington, S. & Stanley, S., 'What Works: Revising the Evidence in England and Wales', in *Probation Journal*, Vol. 52, 2004, pp. 7-20.

Mill, J.S., *Examination of Sir William Hamilton's Philosophy*, London: Longman Green and Company, 1865.

Mill, J.S., *Utilitarianism*, London: Parker, Son and Bourn, 1863.

Mill, J.S., *Collected Works*, [J. Robson Ed.], Toronto: University of Toronto Press, 1991.

Miller, D., *Social Justice*, Oxford: Oxford University Press, 1976.

Miller, D., *Principles of Social Justice*, Cambridge: Harvard University Press, 1999.

Ministry of Justice, *Offender Management Caseload Statistics*, London: Ministry of Justice, 2010.

Ministry of Justice, *Punishment and Reform: Effective Community Sentences*, London: Ministry of Justice, 2012a.

Ministry of Justice, *Statistics on Women in the Criminal justice System 2011*, London: Ministry of Justice, 2012b.

Ministry of Justice, *Prisoners' Childhood and Family Backgrounds*, London: Ministry of Justice, 2012c.

Ministry of Justice, *Restorative Justice Action Plan for the Criminal justice System*, London: Ministry of Justice, 2012d.

Ministry of Justice, *Facing Up to Offending: Restorative Justice in the Criminal justice System*, London: Ministry of Justice, 2012e.

Ministry of Justice, *Getting it Right for Victims and Witnesses*, Consultation Paper, CM8288, London: Ministry of Justice, 2012f.

Ministry of Justice, *Proven Re-offending Quarterly - October 2010 to September 2011*, London: Ministry of Justice, 2013a.

Ministry of Justice, *Story of the Prison Population: 1993-2012 England and Wales*, London: Ministry of Justice, 2013b.

Ministry of Justice, *Costs per Place and Costs per Prisoner*, London: Ministry of Justice, 2013c.

Ministry of Justice, *Proven Re-offending Statistics Quarterly: January 2011to December 2011*, London: Ministry of Justice, 2013d.

Ministry of Justice, *Offender Management Statistics: Prison Population 2014*, London: Ministry of Justice, 2014a.

Ministry of Justice, *Offender Management Statistics Annual Tables 2013*. London: Ministry of Justice, 2014b.

Ministry of Justice, *Offender Management Statistics Quarterly, January to March 2014*, London: Ministry of Justice, 2014c.

Ministry of Justice, *Criminal Justice Statistics Quarterly Update to March 2014*, London: Ministry of Justice, 2014d.

Ministry of Justice, *Offender Management Statistics Quarterly: January to March 2014*, London: Ministry of Justice, 2014e.

Ministry of Justice, *Proven Re-offending Statistics Quarterly: April 2011 to March 2012*, London: Ministry of Justice, 2014f.

Ministry of Justice, *Annual Report and Accounts 2013-2014*, London: Ministry of Justice, 2014g.

Ministry of Justice, *Offender Management Statistics Annual Tables 2014*, London: Ministry of Justice, 2014h.

Mirsky, L., *The Nanaimo Community Justice Forum: A Restorative Justice Partnership in British Columbia, Canada*, International Institute for Restorative Practices, Bethlehem, Pennsylvania, 2005, available at: www.iipr.Edu/article_detail.php?article_id=Mzkx (Accessed 2 February 2015).

Montesquieu, C.-L., *The Spirit of Laws,* Public Domain [tr. T. Nugent], London: G. Bell & Sons, 1914.

Morris, N., *The Future of Imprisonment,* Chicago: University of Chicago Free Press, 1974.

Moore, M.S., 'The Moral Worth of Retribution', in F. Schoeman (Ed.), *Responsibility, Character and the Emotions: New Essays in Moral Psychology,* Cambridge: Cambridge University Press, 1987.

Mundle, C.W.K. (1954), 'Punishment and Desert', in *Philosophical Quarterly,* Vol. iv, No. 16, and also in H.B. Acton (Ed.), *The Philosophy of Punishment: A Collection of Papers,* London: Macmillan, 1969, pp. 65-81.

National Offender Management Service, *Business Plan 2014-2015,* London: NOMS, 2014.

Nussbaum, M., 'Equity and Mercy', in J. Murphy (Ed.), *Punishment and Rehabilitation,* Belmont: Wadsworth, 1995, pp. 212-248.

Office for National Statistics, *Divorces in England and Wales 2009,* Fareham: ONS, 2011.

Office for National Statistics, *Crime in England and Wales – Quarterly First Report (March),* London: ONS, 2012.

Office for National Statistics, *Labour Market Statistics, Tables for 2012 (September),* London: ONS, 2013.

Pincoffs, E., 'Are Questions of Desert Decidable?', in J.B. Cederblom & W. Blizek (Eds.), *Justice and Punishment,* Cambridge: Ballinger, 1977, pp. 75-88.

Plato, 'Laws', in J. Cooper (Ed.) *Plato: Complete Works,* [tr. T.J. Saunders], Indianapolis: Hackett, 1997a.

Plato, 'Republic', in C.D.C. Reeve (Ed.) *Plato Complete Works,* [tr. G.M.A. Grube], Indianapolis: Hackett, 1997b.

Pojman, L., *Justice,* Upper Saddle River: Pearson, 2006.

Pojman, L. & McLeod, O. (Eds.), *What Do We Deserve? A Reader on Justice and Desert,* New York: Oxford University Press, 1999.

Primoratz, I., *Justifying Legal Punishment*, Atlantic Highlands: Humanities Press, 1989.

Prins, H., *Criminal Behaviour*, London: Tavistock, 1982.

Prison Reform Trust, *Bromley Briefings – Prison Factfile,* London: Prison Reform Trust, 2008.

Prison Reform Trust, *Briefing*, 2009, at: www.prisonreformtrust.org.uk (Accessed 5 October 2010)

Prison Reform Trust, *Bromley Briefings*, London: Prison Reform Trust, 2013, available at: www.prisonreformtrust.org.uk/Portals/o/Documents/Factfile%2520autumn%25202013.pdf (Accessed 11 December 2013).

Prison Reform Trust, *Bromley Briefings*, London: Prison Reform Trust, 2014, available at: www.prisonreformtrust.org.uk (Accessed 18 October 2014)

Putnam, R., *Making Democracy Work*, Princeton: Princeton University Press, 1993.

Quinton, A.M., 'On Punishment', in *Analysis*, Vol. 14, No. 6, 1954 (June), and also in H.B. Acton (Ed.), *The Philosophy of Punishment: A Collection of Papers*, London: Macmillan, 1969, pp. 55-64.

Rachels, J., 'What People Deserve', in *Can Ethics Provide Answers? And Other Essays in Moral Philosophy*, Lanham, MD: Rowman and Littlefield, 1997, pp. 175-97.

Rashdall, H., (1891), 'The Theory of Punishment', in *International Journal of Ethics*, 2 (1), 1907, and in *The Theory of Good and Evil*, London: Oxford University Press, 1924.

Rawls, J., 'Two Concepts of Rules', in *Philosophical Review*, Vol. lxiv, 1955 (January), and also in H.B. Acton (Ed.), *The Philosophy of Punishment: A Collection of Papers*, London: Macmillan, 1969, pp. 105-114.

Rawls, J., *A Theory of Justice*, Cambridge, MA: Harvard University Press, 1971.

Rawls, J., in E. Kelly (Ed.), *Justice as Fairness: A Restatement*, Harvard University Press, 2001.

Ross, W.D., *The Right and the Good*, Oxford: Oxford University Press, 1930.

Rutherford, A., *Prisons and the Process of Justice*, Oxford: Oxford University Press, 1986.

Scheffler, S., 'Justice and Desert in Liberal Theory', in *California Law Review*, 88, 2000 (May), pp. 965-990.

Schmidtz, D., 'How to Deserve', *Journal of Political Theory*, Vol. 30, No. 6, 2002 (December), pp. 774-799.

Schuilenberg, M.R., Van Staden, R, & Oude Breuil, R. (Eds.), *Positive Criminology: Reflections on Care, Belonging and Security*, The Hague: Eleven International Publishing, 2014.

Schultz, B., 'Henry Sidgwick', in E.N. Zolta (Ed.), *The Stanford Encyclopedia of Philosophy*, 2012, and at: http://Plato.stanford.Edu/archives/sidgwick/ (Accessed 5 July 2014).

Schumann, H. & Presser, S., *Questions and Answers in Attitude Surveys: Experiments on Question Form, Wording and Context*, New York: Academic Press, 1981.

Scottish Government, *Redesigning the Community Justice System: Response to Consultation*: Edinburgh: Scottish Government, 2013.

Seneca, L.A., 'To Nero On Mercy' [De Clementia], *Moral Essays*, II.ii.2.iv, [tr. J.W. Basore], The Loeb Classical Library, London: Heinemann, (1928-35).

Shapland, J., Atkinson, A., Atkinson, H., Colledge, E., Dignan, J., Howes, M., Johnstone, J., Robibson, G, & Soresby, A., 'Situating Restorative Justice Within Criminal Justice', in *Theoretical Criminology*, Vol. 10, (4), London: Thousand Oaks, SAGE Publications, 2006, pp. 505-532.

Sher, G., *Desert*, Princeton: Princeton University Press, 1987.

Sidgwick, H., (1893), *The Methods of Ethics*, in F.A. Olafson (Ed.), 'The Common Notion of Justice: Analysis and Critique', *Justice and Social Policy*, Englewood Cliffs: Prentice Hall, 1961, pp. 3-28.

Smilansky, S., 'Control, Desert and the Difference Between Distributive and Retributive Justice', in *Philosophical Studies*, 131(3), 2006, pp. 511-524.

Steadman, H.J. & Cocozza, J.J., *Careers of the Criminally Insane: Excessive Social Control of Deviance*, Lexington: D.C. Heath and Company, 1974.

Sterba, J., 'Justice as Desert', *Journal of Social Theory*, 57, 1974, pp. 101-116.

Sterba, J., 'Justice and the Concept of Desert', in *The Personalist*, 57, 1976, pp. 188-197.

Stewart, I., 'Men of Class: Aristotle, Montesquieu and Dicey on "Separation of Powers" and "The Rule of Law"', in *Maquarie Law Journal*, Vol. 4, 2004, pp. 187 *et seq.*

Tak, P., 'Sentencing and Punishment in the Netherlands', in M. Tonry & R.S. Frase (Eds.), *Sentencing and Sanctions in Western Countries*, New York: Oxford University Press, 2001, pp. 151-187.

Tangney, J.P., Stuevig, J. & Hafez, L., 'Shame, Guilt and Remorse: Implications for Offender Populations', in *Journal of Forensic Psychiatry and Psychology*, 22(5), 2011 (September), pp. 706-723.

Ten, C.L., *Crime, Guilt and Punishment*, Oxford: Clarendon Press, 1987.

Tonry, M., 'Evidence, Elections and Ideology in the Making of Criminal justice Policy', in M. Tonry (Ed.), *Confronting Crime: Crime Control Policy Under New Labour*, Devon: Willan Publishing, 2003.

Tonry, M. & Frase, R.S. (Eds.), *Sentencing and Sanctions in Western Countries*, New York: Oxford University Press, 2001.

Travis, A., 'Official Figures Reveal Rising Violence in Prisons in England and Wales', in *The Guardian*, 31 July 2014, London and Manchester: Guardian Newspapers, p. 3.

Urmson, J.O., 'The Interpretation of the Moral Philosophy of J.S. Mill', in *The Philosophical Quarterly*, Vol. 3, No. 10, 1953 (January), pp. 33-39.

Velasquez, M., Andre, C., Shanks, T., Meyer, S.J. & Meyer, J., 'Justice and Fairness', *Issues in Ethics*, Vol. 3, No. 2, 1990 (Spring).

Von Hirsch, A., *Doing Justice: The Choice of Punishments*, New York: Hill and Wang, 1976.

Von Hirsch, A., *Past or Future Crimes: Deservedness and Dangerousness in the Sentencing of Criminals,* Manchester: Manchester University Press, 1985.

Von Hirsch, A., *Censure and Sanctions*, Oxford: Oxford University Press, 1993.

Walgrave, L., *Restorative Justice, Self-Interest and Responsible Citizenship*, Cullompton Devon: Willan Publishing, 2008.

Wechsler, D., 'The Criteria of Criminal Responsibility', in *University of Chicago Law Review*, Vol. 22, 1955, p. 374.

Whitehead, S., *Justice for Sale: The Privatisation of Offender Management Services*, London: TUC, 2014,

Wiegend, T., 'Sentencing and Punishment in Germany', in M. Tonry & R.S. Frase (Eds.), *Sentencing and Sanctions in Western Countries*, New York: Oxford University Press, 2001, pp. 188-221.

Younkins, E, *Justice in a Free Society*, Quebec: Liberty Free Press, 2000, also available at: http://quebecoislibre.org/younkins27.htm (Accessed 10 October 2014).

Wright, M., 'Victim-Offender Mediation as a Step Towards a Restorative System of Justice', in H. Messmer & H.U.Otto (Eds.), *Restorative Justice on Trial: Pitfalls and Potentials of Victim-Offender Mediation*, Dordrecht/Boston: Kluwer Academic Publishers, 1992, pp. 525-539.

Zehr, H., *Changing Lenses: A New Focus for Crime and Justice,* Scottdale: Herald Press, 1990.

Zehr, H., *The Little Book of Restorative Justice*, Intercourse: Good Books, 2002.

Zehr, H. & Mika, H., 'Fundamental Principles of Restorative Justice', in *Contemporary Justice Review*, 1(1), 1998, pp. 47-55.

INDEX

Y

Z